THE COMMON LAW

NUMBER 12

JACKSON & POWELL

ON

PROFESSIONAL NEGLIGENCE

Second Cumulative Supplement
to the
Third Edition

Up-to-date until March 17, 1994

LONDON
SWEET & MAXWELL
1994

Published in 1994 by
Sweet & Maxwell Limited, of South Quay Plaza
183, Marsh Wall, London E14 9FT
Phototypeset by
LBJ Enterprises Ltd. of Aldermaston and Chilcompton
and printed in Great Britain by
The Headway Press Ltd.

No natural products were destroyed to make this product. Only farmed
timber was used and replanted.

A catalogue record for this book is available from the British Library

ISBN Main Work   0–421–45930 1

Supplement ISBN 0–421–52120 1

HOW TO USE THIS SUPPLEMENT

This is the Second Cumulative Supplement to the Third Edition of
Jackson and Powell on Professional Negligence, and has been compiled
according to the structure of the main volume.

At the beginning of each chapter of this Supplement the mini table of
contents from the main volume has been included. Where a heading in
this table of contents has been marked by the symbol ■, the material
under that heading has been added to or amended, and should be
referred to.

Within each chapter, updating information is referenced to the relevant
paragraph in the main volume.

TABLE OF CASES

(vii)

TABLE OF STATUTES

TABLE OF STATUTORY INSTRUMENTS

RULES OF THE SUPREME COURT

CHAPTER 1

GENERAL

3.—TORTIOUS LIABILITY

(i) The Tort of Negligence

(b) *Theoretical basis for the duty of care*

Duties owed by public authorities

Add: In *Lonrho* v. *Tebbit* [1991] 4 All E.R. 973 the Vice-Chancellor **1–30** refused to strike out a claim against the Secretary of State for Trade and Industry in relation to the exercise of his powers under the Fair Trading Act 1973. The Vice-Chancellor considered it arguable that the relevant decision was operational rather than one of policy. He took the view that the issues raised were justiciable. The Court of Appeal upheld that decision, although observing that the plaintiff faced considerable difficulties in its claim: [1992] 4 All E.R. 280, C.A.

Developments in 1990: *Murphy* v. *Brentwood District Council*

Add to NOTE 6: This decision and indeed the line of appellate decisions **1–39** leading up to it are strongly criticised by Markesinis and Deakin in "The

Random Element of Their Lordship's Infallible Judgment: An Economic and Comparative Analysis of the Tort of Negligence from *Anns* to *Murphy*" (1992) 55 M.L.R. 619.

Insert new paragraph after § 1–41:

Developments in 1991

1–41A   The courts have embarked on the not inconsiderable task of working out the implications of *Murphy* v. *Brentwood District Council* [1991] 1 A.C. 398. In *Nitrigin Eireann Teoranta* v. *Inco Alloys Ltd.* [1992] 1 W.L.R. 498 May J. had to reconsider *Pirelli* v. *Oscar Faber & Partners* [1983] 2 A.C. 1 and *Junior Books* v. *Veitchi* [1983] 1 A.C. 520 in the light of *Murphy*. The first defendant, a specialist manufacturer, supplied piping for the plaintiff's chemical production plant in 1981 pursuant to contract. In 1983 cracking occurred, which the plaintiff took reasonable steps to repair. On June 27, 1984 the piping cracked again and an explosion occurred. It was assumed for the trial of the preliminary issues (though denied by the first defendant) that the piping was defective and had cracked because of negligence in manufacture. The writ was issued on June 21, 1990 (by which date any contractual claim would have been long since statute-barred). On a trial of preliminary issues May J. held: (1) The first defendant had no liability for the cracking in 1983. That was pure economic loss. *Pirelli* (where it was assumed that the defendants had tortious liability in respect of cracking to the chimney) was distinguished, because the defendant in that case, unlike the first defendant in the instant case, was a professional firm. May J. felt unable to distinguish *Junior Books*, but he declined to apply it (see p. 505B–C). (2) The first defendants incurred liability in tort for the first time on June 27, 1984 when damage occurred to "other property" as a result of the explosion. Therefore the plaintiffs' claim in tort was not statute-barred.

1–41B   The decision in *Nitrigin* would certainly seem to be a correct application of the principles enunciated in *Murphy*. However, it does highlight the anomalous position of *Junior Books*. It also points up the potential conflict between the reasoning in *Murphy* and *Pirelli* (discussed at § 1–113 of the main volume), which still has to be resolved. These issues are further discussed by A. McGee in "Back to *Pirelli*" (1992) 108 L.Q.R. 364 and by R.A. O'Dair in "Professional Negligence: Some Further Limiting Factors" (1992) 55 M.L.R. 405.

Subsequent cases on economic loss

1–41C   A particular problem thrown up by *Murphy* is the extent of negligence liability for economic loss in situations outside the *Hedley Byrne* relationship. This has recently been considered by the Court of Appeal in three cases: *Spring* v. *Guardian Assurance plc* [1993] 2 All E.R. 273, *White* v. *Jones* [1993] 3 W.L.R. 730 and *Preston* v. *Torfaen Borough Council* [1993] C.I.L.L. 857. In *Spring* v. *Guardian Assurance plc* the Court of Appeal held that the giver of a reference does not owe to the person the subject of the reference a duty of care either (i) in giving or compiling the reference or (ii) in obtaining the information on which it is based. The reasoning was that the plaintiff's remedy (if any) lay in the tort of defamation and it was not fair, just or reasonable to impose a duty of care in tort. This decision may be thought correct in principle, but it has been strongly criticised by Weir ("The Case of the Careless Referee" (1993) 52 C.L.J. 376) and is now under appeal to the House of Lords. In *White* v. *Jones* (discussed in this supplement at § 4–25A) the Court of Appeal held that a solicitor instructed to prepare a will owes a duty of care to the intended beneficiaries. This too is under appeal to the House of Lords. In *Preston* v. *Torfaen Borough Council* (discussed in this supplement at § 2–48A) the Court of Appeal proceeded on the basis that liability for economic loss outside the *Hedley Byrne* situation was restricted to a small number of exceptional categories of case (into which the instant case did not fall). Thus the trend towards restricting tortious liability for economic loss, at least in this country, continues unabated.

The Commonwealth reaction to Murphy

The House of Lords' reasoning in *Murphy* was inspired, or at least **1–41D** heavily influenced, by the High Court of Australia, as discussed in paragraph 1–39 of the main volume. The same issues have now been reconsidered at the highest appellate level in both New Zealand and Canada. In neither jurisdiction has the English/Australian approach found favour.

New Zealand

In *South Pacific Manufacturing Co. Ltd.* v. *New Zealand Security* **1–41E** *Consultants & Investigations Ltd.* [1992] 2 N.Z.L.R. 282 two actions were brought against the agents of insurers for alleged negligence in investigating fires. In the first case the plaintiff was the creditor and principal shareholder of the insured who had lost property in the fire. In the second case the plaintiff was the insured who had suffered losses as a result of the fire. In each case the insurers, relying upon the investigations and report of their agents, had refused to pay out. The New Zealand Court of Appeal held that both actions should be struck out. In neither case did the investigators for the insurers owe a duty of care to the plaintiffs. All five judges favoured a modified version of the *Anns* two-stage test (see § 1–27 of the main volume). Cooke P. (with whom Hardie Boys J. agreed) formulated the correct approach in 15 propositions, set out at pp. 294–299. These propositions represent a thoughtful refinement of the

Anns test and a formidable critique of *Murphy*. It is fair to point out, however, that the actual decision in *South Pacific* would have been precisely the same whether a *Murphy* approach, an *Anns* approach or a modified *Anns* approach had been adopted.

Canada

1–41F   In *Canadian National Railway Co.* v. *Norsk Pacific Steamship Co.* (1992) 91 D.L.R. (4th) 289 the plaintiff railways company was the principal user, but not the owner, of a bridge negligently damaged by the defendant. The plaintiff claimed its economic loss suffered through re-routing traffic while the bridge was being repaired. The Supreme Court of Canada, by a majority of 4:3, held that the plaintiff was entitled to recover. The principal judgment for the majority was given by McLachlin J. with whom L'Heureux-Dubé and Cory JJ. concurred. McLachlin J. defined the underlying problem as the search for a principled mechanism to limit liability for foreseeable economic loss flowing from negligence. He reviewed the different approaches adopted in the principal civil and common law jurisdictions. He rejected the House of Lords' approach in *Murphy*, which achieved doctrinal tidiness or logical precision at the expense of justice. He considered that the Canadian Supreme Court's approach in *City of Kamloops* v. *Nielson* (1984) 10 D.L.R. (4th) 641 (local authority liable for negligent inspection of foundations: *Anns* v. *Merton* applied) was to be preferred. He considered that the crucial issues were (a) proximity and (b) whether there were any residual policy considerations which called for a limitation on liability. Adopting this approach, he considered a duty of care had been established in the instant case. See further this supplement at §2–36A. The Canadian Supreme Court adopted a similar approach to the duty of care issue in *Edgeworth Construction Ltd.* v. *N. D. Lea & Associates* [1993] 8 W.W.R. 129, discussed in this supplement at § 2–53A. This case would probably have been decided differently in England: see *Pacific Associates Inc.* v. *Baxter* [1990] 1 Q.B. 993.

Review of the present dichotomy

1–41G   The problem identified at §§ 1–21 and 1–42 of the main volume is no nearer solution. Broadly speaking, the Australian and British courts have adopted a restrictive approach, while the New Zealand and Canadian courts have adopted a more expansive/flexible approach. This dichotomy becomes more complex, since New Zealand (unlike Australia) still retains appeals to the Privy Council. Unsurprisingly, the Privy Council has reversed a number of recent New Zealand decisions in this area. In *Deloitte Haskins and Sells* v. *National Mutual Life Nominees Ltd.* [1993] A.C. 774 the Privy Council reversed the unanimous decision of the New

Zealand courts that auditors acting under section 50 of the Securities Act 1978 owed any relevant tortious duty to the trustee appointed under the same Act. In *Clarke Boyce* v. *Mouat* [1993] 3 W.L.R. 1021 the Privy Council rejected the proposition that the appellant solicitors owed a tortious or fiduciary duty to tender certain advice to a prospective client before accepting a retainer. In *Downsview Nominees Ltd.* v. *First City Corporation* [1993] A.C. 295 the Privy Council, while upholding the substantive decision, rejected the New Zealand view that a receiver and manager, who elects to carry on the business of the company, owes a duty of care to subsequent debenture holders.

Where next?

Experience over the next few years will indicate which of the above **1–41H** approaches is the more satisfactory and (as the use of comparative law increases) may lead to convergence of the English, Australian, New Zealand and Canadian courts in due course. In all four jurisdictions the underlying common law principles are, or should be, the same and the practical problems faced are remarkably similar. It is suggested that the commentary at §§ 1–42 to 1–49 of the main volume remains valid despite the wealth of recent appellate authority on this intractable topic.

The relevant principles

Add to NOTE 41: *Bonthrone* v. *Secretary of State for Scotland*, 1987 **1–45** S.L.T. 34.

General comment on the 12 principles

Add: For example, the weight which attaches to principle (v) has **1–47** increased substantially in recent years: "The strong trend of recent authority has been to narrow the range of circumstances which the law will recognise as sufficient to impose on one person a duty of care to protect another from damage which consists in purely economic loss" *per* Lord Bridge in *Scally* v. *Southern Health & Social Services Board* [1992] 1 A.C. 294, 304A. See also §1–41C above.

The question of proximity

Add: In cases of physical damage (as opposed to economic loss) **1–48** proximity may still be a relevant criterion where there is no direct contact between the plaintiff and the defendant: *The "Nicholas H"* [1992] 2 Lloyd's Rep. 481.

Add to NOTE 49: A similar approach was adopted in relation to a claim against auditors in the New Zealand case *Fletcher* v. *National Mutual Life Nominees Ltd.* [1990] 3 N.Z.L.R. 641. Henry J., following the approach in *Caparo*, analysed what was the purpose of the provisions of the Securities Act 1978 imposing duties on auditors.

The "just and reasonable" question

1–49   Add to NOTE 57: But see the article by Markesinis and Deakin cited in n. 39 above. It is argued that appellate courts should make more use of techniques of economic analysis, comparative law and, generally, the writings of academic lawyers.

(ii) Concurrent Liability

Authority

1–54   Add: In *The Lloyd's Litigation: The Merrett, Gooda Walker and Feltrim Cases* (December 13, 1993), the Court of Appeal held that managing agents, who were also members' agents, owed concurrent duties both in contract and tort to Lloyd's Names.

Insert new paragraph after § 1–55:

1–55A   One recent first instance decision concerning architects, which effectively rejects concurrent liability, is *Lancashire and Cheshire Association of Baptist Churches Inc.* v. *Howard & Seddon Partnership* [1993] 3 All E.R. 467. This is discussed in this Supplement at § 2–19. For the reasons there set out, it is suggested that that decision may be wrong.

The opposite view

1–57   Add to NOTE 82: However, the editor of *Keating*, in his judicial capacity, has acknowledged that the weight of authority presently favours concurrent liability, and that these more general arguments would only be open in the House of Lords: see *Nitrigin Eireann Teoranta* v. *Inco Alloys Ltd.* [1992] 1 W.L.R. 498, 503G.

(iii) Liability to Third Parties

The construction professions

1–61   Add: The substantial restriction of third party liability following *Murphy* is illustrated by the decision of Judge Newey Q.C. in *Hiron* v. *Pynford South*, 60 B.L.R. 78.

Insurance brokers

1–63   Add: The decision of the Court of Appeal in *Verderame* v. *Commercial Union Assurance* [1992] BCLC 793 reflects the more restrictive approach towards third party liability of insurance brokers, following *Caparo Industries* v. *Dickman* [1990] 2 A.C. 605 and the other major appellate decisions discussed in §§ 1–31—1–41 above.

(iv) Immunity

1–67   Add: In *Palmer* v. *Durnford Ford* [1992] 1 Q.B. 483, Mr. Simon Tuckey Q.C. held on a striking-out application that an expert witness' immunity from suit was restricted to the giving of evidence in court and to "what could fairly be said to be preliminary to his giving evidence in court judged perhaps by the principal purpose for which the work was done" (at p. 488H). See also the discussion of this decision in *Walpole* v. *Partridge & Wilson* [1993] 3 W.L.R. 1093 at pp. 1107–1109.

Add to NOTE 16: The Court of Appeal in *Ancell* v. *McDermott* [1993] R.T.R. 235 applied the same two strands of reasoning as the House of Lords in *Hill*. An action against the police for alleged negligence in failing to protect road users following a spillage of diesel fuel on the road was dismissed on two grounds, namely (i) no relevant duty of care to members of the public, (ii) immunity.

5.—SHARED RESPONSIBILITY

(ii) Contributory Negligence

Add: The New Zealand Court of Appeal considered these questions **1–84** *obiter* in *Mouat* v. *Clarke Boyce* [1992] 2 N.Z.L.R. 559 in relation to the New Zealand Contributory Negligence Act 1947. They favoured the approach adopted by the English Court of Appeal: see the judgment of Cooke P. at p. 564. Although the underlying decision on liability has now been reversed (see [1993] 3 W.L.R. 1021), this separate judgment on contributory negligence was not considered by the Privy Council.

Insert new paragraph after § 1–85:

Deceit
The plea of contributory negligence is not available in answer to a **1–85A** claim for deceit. See *Alliance & Leicester* v. *Edgestop Ltd.* [1993] 1 W.L.R. 1462. In an appropriate case, therefore, an anticipated plea of contributory negligence can be forestalled by pleading the claim in deceit.

8.—LIMITATION OF ACTIONS

(i) The limitation period

Characterising the claim
Add: Section 11 of the Limitation Act 1980 does not apply to actions **1–103** for trepass to the person, even where the consequence is personal injury. Accordingly the limitation period for such claims is six years, and the court has no discretion to extend that period: *Stubbings* v. *Webb* [1993] A.C. 498.

[7]

(iii) Date when Cause of Action in Tort Accrues

(a) *Claims against architects and engineers*

Effect of Murphy on Pirelli

1–113   Add: An alternative view which has been canvassed by some commentators is that the reconciliation of *Murphy* and *Pirelli* requires the substitution of the date of discoverability for the date of occurrence of damage, as the date when "damage" occurs. In other words, it is said that the start date has been pushed forwards rather than backwards. See Mullany, "Limitation of Actions and Latent Damage" (1991) 54 M.L.R. 216 at pp. 227–228; McKendrick, "*Pirelli* Re-examined" (1991) 11 *Journal of Legal Studies* 326 at pp. 335–336; Mullany, "Limitation of Actions—Where are We Now?" [1993] L.M.C.L.Q. 34 at p. 43.

(c) *Claims against solicitors*

Insert new paragraph after § 1–117:

The Australian view

1–117A   The *Forster* v. *Outred & Co.* line of cases discussed in the preceding paragraph were reviewed in some detail by the High Court of Australia in *Wardley Australia Ltd.* v. *Western Australia* (1992) 66 A.L.R. 839. The plaintiff in that case gave an indemnity in 1987 in reliance on representations made by the defendants. In 1989 the plaintiff was called upon to make payment pursuant to the indemnity. In 1991 the plaintiff sought to amend its statement of claim by adding a statutory claim (for which there was a three-year limitation period) to the effect that it had been induced to give the indemnity by the defendant's misleading representations. The High Court held that the plaintiff suffered loss when it was called upon to pay, *not* when it entered into the indemnity agreement. Therefore the amendment was made within the limitation period and should not be struck out. Four of the seven members of the court gave a single judgment to the following effect: where P enters into a contract which exposes him to a contingent liability, he does not suffer damage until the contingency is fulfilled. If (contrary to the analysis at pp. 844–845) *Forster* v. *Outred & Co.* and the other English cases contradict this principle, then they ought not to be followed. It is unreasonable to expect P to commence proceedings before the contingency is fulfilled. Moreover, if damages are assessed on a contingency basis, they might not be adequate.

(iv) Effect of the Latent Damage Act 1986

1–125   Add: In *Société Commerciale de Réassurance* v. *E.R.A.S. (International) Ltd.* [1992] 2 All E.R. 82 (Note) the Court of Appeal held, with regret, that section 14A of the Limitation Act 1980 applied only to actions for the tort of negligence. It did not apply to claims framed in contract.

(v) Special Rules re Personal Injury and Death

(a) *Primary limitation period*

Personal injuries
Add: In *Nash* v. *Eli Lilly & Co.* [1993] 1 W.L.R. 782 the Court of **1–126**
Appeal considered the construction and application of section 14(1) in detail. "Knowledge" in section 14(1) means;

> "condition of mind which imports a degree of certainty and the degree of certainty which is appropriate for this purpose is that which, for the particular plaintiff, may reasonably be regarded as sufficient to justify embarking upon the preliminaries to the making of a claim for compensation such as the taking of legal or other advice." (At p. 792C–D.)

The court discussed at some length the difference between knowledge and belief. If a plaintiff held a firm belief that his injury was attributable to an act or omission by the defendant, but he thought it necessary to obtain reassurance or confirmation by experts, then he would not be regarded as having "knowledge" until his enquiries were (or ought to have been) completed (at p. 795). The meaning of the word "attributable" in the context of section 14 was considered at pp. 797–799.

(b) *Discretionary exclusion of time limit*

Manner in which the discretion is exercised
Add: This question was further considered by the Court of Appeal in **1–130**
Hartley v. *Birmingham District Council* [1992] 1 W.L.R. 968. The writ in a personal injuries action was issued one day late owing to negligence by the plaintiff's solicitors. The Court of Appeal decided to disapply the time limit pursuant to section 33 of the Limitation Act 1980. One important consideration was the prejudice which the plaintiff would suffer, if suing her own solicitor rather than the original tortfeasor. The new defendant, *i.e.* the plaintiff's own solicitor, would know much more about the weak points of her case than the original defendant. See Parker L.J. at p. 980D–E and Leggatt L.J. at p. 983D–E.
Add to NOTE 64: See also the decision of the Court of Appeal in *Nash* v. *Eli Lilly & Co.* [1993] 1 W.L.R. 782. There is extensive discussion of the exercise of discretion under section 33 at pp. 801–809.

9.—INVESTMENT BUSINESS

Add new paragraphs after § 1–138:

Liability of professional persons "knowingly concerned" in breaches of the Financial Services Act 1986

1–139   Section 6(2) of F.S.A. 1986 provides:

> "If, on the application of the Secretary of State [who has now delegated his powers to the S.I.B.], the court is satisfied that a person has entered into any transaction in contravention of section 3 above [which is set out in § 1–136] the court may order that person and any other person who appears to the court to have been knowingly concerned in the contravention to take such steps as the court may direct for restoring the parties to the position in which they were before the transaction was entered into."

Section 61(1)(c) sets out very similar rights in respect of breaches of other provisions of the F.S.A. and rules made thereunder. The reference to persons "knowingly concerned" can plainly include professional advisers, such as solicitors and accountants.

1–140   In *S.I.B.* v. *Pantell S.A. (No. 2)* [1993] Ch. 256 the S.I.B. brought an action under sections 6 and 61 against two overseas companies for various breaches of the F.S.A. 1986, in particular for carrying on investment business in the U.K., not being authorised to do so, and causing investors loss. The S.I.B. joined as third, fourth and fifth defendants solicitors who had acted for the companies and, allegedly, had been "knowingly concerned" in the companies' breaches of the F.S.A.

On the solicitors' application to strike out the claims, the Vice-Chancellor held:

(*a*) Sections 6(2) and 61(1) provide for a statutory rescission of an unlawful transaction. The court can order the contravener to repay the monies paid to him under the unlawful transaction.

(*b*) Under those sections the court can make the same order against third parties knowingly concerned in the contravention. Accordingly the Vice-Chancellor dismissed the application to strike out.

He accordingly granted a declaration that the court had jurisdiction to order the solicitors, if they had been knowingly concerned in a relevant contravention by Pantell, to pay to investors sums equivalent to those paid to Pantell. The Court of Appeal dismissed an appeal by the solicitors. The Court held that it was irrelevant that the persons knowingly concerned had received nothing under the impugned transactions. For further discussion of this decision see Lomnika [1993] J.B.L. 54.

CHAPTER 2

ARCHITECTS, ENGINEERS AND QUANTITY SURVEYORS

1.—GENERAL

Add to NOTE 5: In a Report entitled *Review of the Architects* **2-03** *(Registration) Acts 1931–1969* (H.M.S.O., 1993), Mr. E. J. D. Warne C.B., an assessor for the Department of the Environment, has recommended that the statutory protection of the title "architect" should be abolished and the Architects Registration Council for the United Kingdom should be disbanded on the grounds that statutory protection for architects is anomalous, out-moded and not in the public interest.

(i) Duties to Client

(b) *Duties independent of contract*

Duties imposed by statute

Delete sub-paragraph (v) and substitute: **2–18**

(v) There is a question of construction as to whether the Act imposes separate duties to carry out work (*a*) in a workmanlike or professional manner, (*b*) with proper materials and (*c*) so that the dwelling will be fit for habitation when completed or whether the requirement of fitness for habitation is a measure of the standard required in the performance of the duty imposed by section 1(1). In *Thompson* v. *Clive Alexander & Partners*,[58] His Honour Judge Esyr Lewis Q.C. considered this matter and held the latter construction to be correct. He based his reasoning first on statements by members of the Court of Appeal in *Alexander* v. *Mercouris*[58a] and secondly on his view that the plain intention of the Act was only to ensure that dwellings were built in such a way as to ensure that they were fit for habitation on completion. The decision is somewhat difficult to reconcile both with the words of the statute and with observations by Buckley and Goff L.JJ. in *Alexander* v. *Mercouris* that a cause of action would arise during the course of construction once bad workmanship had taken place (although it appears to have been implicit that the bad workmanship would be such as to render the dwelling unfit for habitation if and when the dwelling was completed). If correct, the decision imposes a further significant limit on the scope of the Act.

Add:

(viii) A dwelling will be unfit for habitation when completed notwithstanding that a defect is latent rather than patent. In *Andrews* v. *Schooling*,[60a] Balcombe L.J. said:

> "If, when the work is completed, the dwelling is without some essential attribute—*e.g.* a roof or a damp course—it may well be unfit for human habitation even though the problems resulting from the lack of that attribute have not then become patent. A house without a roof is unfit for habitation even though it does not rain until some months after the house has been completed."

NOTE 58. (1992) 28 Con.L.R. 49.
NOTE 58a. [1979] 1 W.L.R. 1270.
NOTE 60a. [1991] 1 W.L.R. 783, C.A. at p. 790.

Duties imposed at common law

2–19 Add to NOTE 64: *Hiron* v. *Pynford South Ltd.* is now reported at 60 B.L.R. 78. For brief facts see supplement to § 2–46, below. Although His Honour Judge Newey Q.C. found that the mere existence of a contract was insufficient to prevent a concurrent duty, he rejected such a concurrent duty unless it added to the normal implied contractual term to exercise reasonable skill and care, stating (at p. 717):

"Since the Legal & General and [the engineers] had entered into an express contract whereby [the engineers] were to advise the Legal & General in return for payment and a duty in tort to take care in giving advice would merely have duplicated an implied term in contract, I do not think that it was just and reasonable that [the engineers] should have owed a duty in tort. The only probable result of adding a tortious obligation would have been to have given the Legal & General a longer period in which to sue [the engineers] but if that had been the intention of the parties they could have provided for it in their contract. The position would have been different if contractual and tortious duties had not precisely coincided."

By contrast, May J. has accepted that it is only in the House of Lords that it would be possible to argue that a professional person did not owe a duty of care to a client with whom the professional is in contract: see *Nitrigin Eireann Teoranta* v. *Inco Alloys Ltd.* [1992] 1 W.L.R. 498 at p. 503G.

Add new NOTE 64a after last sentence: The conceptual difficulties which occur when evaluating the nature and extent of concurrent duties of care are illustrated by the decision of His Honour Judge Kershaw Q.C. in *Lancashire and Cheshire Association of Baptist Churches Inc.* v. *Howard & Seddon Partnership (A firm)* [1993] 3 All E.R. 467. The defendant architects undertook an unusual role in that they were also for all practical purposes the contractor controlling and supervising the construction of the works to the plaintiff's church. It was accepted, for the purposes of a preliminary issue, that the plaintiff's claim in contract in respect of design defects was statute-barred although the claim in negligence was not. The Judge found (1) that there could be a duty of care even though the parties were in a contractual relationship; (2) that the loss suffered by the plaintiffs was economic; and (3) that as a result there was no duty of care to avoid economic loss. The first conclusion is unexceptionable. It is, however, respectfully submitted that the third conclusion did not follow from the second. The vast majority of claims by clients against professional men will be for "pure" economic loss. It is submitted that the nature of the loss is only one factor to be taken into account in determining whether or not a duty of care is owed in a particular factual situation. Where all other factors point to the existence of such a duty, the nature of the loss should not prevent it regardless of whether or not the parties are in a contractual relationship. See further Chap. 1, §§ 1–50—1–56, and supplement.

Add: In *Rowlands* v. *Collow*,[70a] Thomas J. found an engineer to be **2–21** concurrently liable for the design of a driveway in contract and tort and refused to follow the decision of the New Zealand Court of Appeal in

McLaren Maycroft & Co. v. *Fletcher Development Co. Ltd.*[70b] which had held that a claim for negligence in the performance of professional services was a claim in contract and contract only. The Judge did so on the basis of decisions in other Commonwealth jurisdictions and, in particular, *Central Trust Company* v. *Rafuse.*[70c] He stated:

> "There is no doubt that the decisions and literature are over-whelmingly in favour of concurrent liability. I venture to suggest that this preponderance of support for concurrent liability reflects the merits of the competing arguments. The issue is now virtually incontestable; a person who has performed professional services may be held liable concurrently in contract and in negligence unless the terms of the contract preclude the tortious liability."

Similarly, in *Pullen* v. *Gutteridge*,[70d] the Court of Appeal of Victoria rejected a submission that an architect did not owe a duty of care to his client in respect of economic losses. The Court summarised the position in Australia as follows[70e]:

> ". . . ever since *Voli* v. *Inglewood Shire Council* (1963) 110 C.L.R. 74 it has been clear that an architect or engineer may be liable to his client in tort as well as in contract. We refer also to *Macpherson & Kelley* v. *Kevin J. Prunty & Associates* [1983] 1 V.R. 573, especially at p. 580, *per* Lush J., where it is said that the view is no longer tenable that concurrent liability in tort exists only where some physical injury or damage is likely to result. Moreover, it is apparent that the matter of 'reliance', which will often be important in determining the existence of relevant proximity, need not be pleaded or proved where there is a relationship of a professional man and his client. A duty of care is implicit in such a relationship, as is perhaps reliance itself: *Sutherland Shire Council* v. *Heyman* (1985) 157 C.L.R. 424 at pp. 497 and 502 *per* Deane J. It is, in any event, manifest beyond argument that the appellant, as a client, in fact relied on the respondent as the designer of the centre."

NOTE 70a. [1992] 1 N.Z.L.R. 178.
NOTE 70b. [1973] 2 N.Z.L.R. 100.
NOTE 70c. [1986] 2 S.C.R. 147: a decision concerning solicitors. See further Chap. 4, § 4–09.
NOTE 70d. [1993] 1 V.R. 27.
NOTE 70e. *Ibid.* at pp. 39–40.

Importance of concurrent liability

2–26   Add to NOTE 84: See also the discussion of *Hiron* v. *Pynford South Ltd.* 60 B.L.R. 78; (1992) 28 E.G. 112; [1992] C.I.L.L. 716, in the supplement to n. 64 in § 2–19, above.

(ii) Duties to Third Parties

(a) *The nature of the damage suffered will be relevant to although not determinative of the existence of a duty of care to prevent that damage*

Add on p. 104, line 8 after "Local Authority" a new NOTE 11a: A local **2–34** authority will, however, be liable for personal injuries suffered by a tenant as a result of a design defect in a house even if the tenant knew of the defect provided that it would not have been reasonable for the tenant to remedy the defect: *Targett* v. *Torfaen B.C.* [1992] 3 All E.R. 27; [1992] P.I.Q.R. P125, discussed further in the supplement to § 2–40, below.

Add new NOTE 20a at the end of the paragraph: An argument that a **2–35** geotechnical engineer engaged by the vendor of the property to provide advice concerning the ground beneath the property was responsible to the purchaser for damage to the property was rejected by Newbury J. at first instance in British Columbia in *Sergius* v. *Janax Design & Drafting* (1992) 64 B.C.L.R. (2d) 176. The judge stated at p. 198:

> "Although not without its attractions, this argument overlooks the fact that those cases denying recovery for pure economic loss are concerned not so much with the nature of the damage as with the fact that the plaintiff is seeking to recover the cost of repairing a defective product which has been supplied or sold by a person against whom the plaintiff has no warranty in contract. The law's reluctance to create contract-like warranties in favour of such a plaintiff, rather than any distinction in principle based on the type of damage *per se*, is at the heart of the rule against recovery."

Insert a new paragraph after § 2–36:

The extent to which *Anns* is good law in other Commonwealth **2–36A** jurisdictions is now under active consideration. By refusing to follow *Anns*,[21a] the High Court of Australia re-emphasised the traditional limitations on the recovery of economic loss in tort. However it is not clear that the Australian courts are ready to retreat as far from *Anns* as the English courts are now doing. In *National Mutual Life Association of Australasia Ltd.* v. *Coffey & Partners Pty. Ltd.*,[21b] the Queensland Court of Appeal refused to strike out a claim by subsequent purchasers of a property for the cost of repairing cracks in the foundations against engineers instructed by the original owner and builder of the property on the basis that there was a serious question as to whether the subsequent purchaser had placed reliance on the original engineers. In *Opat* v. *National Mutual Life Association of Australasia Ltd.*,[21c] Southwell J. at first instance in Victoria on the hearing of a preliminary issue, held that a builder could, in certain circumstances be liable for economic losses to future purchasers who were unidentified by name. However, he held that it would be necessary to plead and prove reliance by such purchasers in order to establish the necessary proximity for a duty of care to arise. It is not clear from either of the Australian cases as to what, precisely, would be required in order to establish the necessary "reliance" although it appears that some form of negligent statement or misrepresentation might be required.

The position is similarly unclear in Canada. In *Canadian National Railway Co.* v. *Norsk Pacific Steamship Co. (The Jervis Crown)*,[21d] the Canadian Supreme Court found a barge operator who negligently damaged a bridge liable for economic losses incurred by the operator of a railway which had the right to use, but did not own, the bridge. In *British Columbia Hydro & Power Authority* v. *N.D. Lea & Associates* (1992) 69 B.C.L.R. (2d) 309, 336,[21e] Newbury J. attempted an analysis of the judgments of the court as follows:

> "The three judgments in *Jervis Crown* have made the analysis of cases involving economic loss much more complicated. Except perhaps for the confirmation of *Anns* by four members of the court, the judgments do not provide a true ratio, nor even a specific approach to economic loss approved by a majority of the seven judges. McLachlin J. with whom L'Hereux-Dubé and Sopinka JJ. concurred, applied *Anns* and found the *proximity* between the plaintiff and the owner of the damaged property was such as to bring the case within the ambit of the "common venture" line of maritime cases where recovery of economic loss has been allowed in the past. Stevenson J. and La Forest J. (with whom Iacobucci and Corey JJ. concurred), both rejected proximity as a useful test for liability because it 'expresses a conclusion, a judgment, a result, rather than a principle', but Stevenson J. applying a 'known plaintiff rule,' concurred with McLachlin J. in allowing recovery. La Forest J., who would have dismissed the plaintiff's claim, preferred to limit his reasons to the subclass of economic loss cases involving 'relational economic loss.' In respect of that category he found that there were policy reasons for the longstanding 'bright line rule' against recovery, and no sound policy reasons for departing from the rule in the case before the court."

At the end of his judgment, Newbury J. stated that because of the lack of a clear *ratio*, the defendant was seeking a re-hearing of the appeal before the full Court. In the earlier decision of *University of Regina* v. *Pettick*[21f] the Saskatchewan Court of Appeal, refused to follow *Murphy* and stated that *Anns* was still good law in Canada.[21g]

The Courts in New Zealand have consistently refused to follow either the principles set out in *Murphy* or the actual result in the case. In *South*

Pacific Manufacturing Co. Ltd. v. *New Zealand Consultants & Investigations Ltd.*,[21h] the New Zealand Court of Appeal stated that negligence law in New Zealand had not changed as a result of the decision. In *Otago Cheese Co. Ltd.* v. *Nick Stoop Builders Ltd.*[21i] (claim against a local authority for economic loss) Fraser J. stated:

> "The existence and general nature of the duty which arises in this sort of case is now well established . . . this district council was under a duty to take reasonable care: (1) in deciding whether the plans complied with the bylaws or were deficient in some respect; (2) in deciding whether and when to exercise its power to inspect; and (3) in carrying out any such inspection."[21j]

NOTE 21a. In *Sutherland Shire Council* v. *Heyman* (1985) 157 C.L.R. 424.

NOTE 21b. [1991] 2 Qd.R. 401; a decision after *D. & F. Estates Ltd.* v. *Church Commissioners for England* [1989] A.C. 177 but prior to *Murphy* v. *Brentwood D.C.* [1991] 1 A.C. 398.

NOTE 21c. [1992] 1 V.R. 283; a decision after *Murphy*.

NOTE 21d. (1992) 137 N.R. 241.

NOTE 21e. For facts see new § 2–59A, below.

NOTE 21f. (1991) 77 D.L.R. (4th) 615.

NOTE 21g. See further the supplement to § 2–50, below.

NOTE 21h. [1992] 2 N.Z.L.R. 282 (claims by assured for negligence against a professional fire investigators employed by insurer struck out as disclosing no reasonable cause of action).

NOTE 21i. Unreported (Dunedin, CP 180/89, May 18, 1992).

NOTE 21j. Applied and followed by Williamson J. in *Hamlin* v. *Bruce Stirling Ltd.* [1993] 1 N.Z.L.R. 374 at p. 380.

(b) *Loss claimed against a building professional as a result of defects in a structure in respect of which he has been engaged will generally be treated as irrecoverable economic loss save where the "complex structure" theory applies*

Add to NOTE 22: See also the first instance decision by Newbury J. in **2–37** British Columbia, *Sergius* v. *Janax Design & Drafting* (1992) 64 B.C.L.R. (2d) 176 where he rejected a claim by a purchaser against an engineer originally retained by a vendor for the cost of repairing defects in a property on the grounds that there was no sufficient relationship of proximity. On similar facts Hutchison J., another puisne Judge in British Columbia, also rejected a claim for economic losses sustained by a subsequent purchaser against a geotechnical engineer employed by an earlier owner in *British Columbia Ltd.* v. *HMT Agra Ltd.* (1993) 82 B.C.L.R. (2d) 203. The defendant had prepared a report which was, without the defendant's consent or knowledge, annexed to a restrictive covenant and filed in the land registry. The Judge found that although the plaintiff was able to establish that he had relied on the report it was not foreseeable to the defendant that such reliance would take place with the result that no duty of care arose.

Protection from liability to third parties

2–39   Add to NOTE 28: Such a claim has now been allowed by His Honour Judge O'Donoghue sitting as a Judge of the High Court, in *Morse* v. *Barratt (Leeds) Limited* (1993) 9 Con. L.J. 158, Ch.D. The plaintiffs, who were largely subsequent purchasers of houses, joined together to re-build an old wall which had been rendered dangerous by the action of the defendant, the original builder of the houses. The Judge found that the claim fell squarely within Lord Bridge's suggested qualification.

In an article "Has Construction Law Been Taken to the Wreckers?" (1991) 65 A.L.J. 270, 274, P. Gerber and R. Jackson point out that although a person may be obliged, if he is not to be liable in nuisance, to remedy a mischief on his own land once he is aware of the same, it does not follow that he is entitled to recover the cost of remedy from the author of the mischief.

(c) *A building professional engaged to undertake work will owe a duty to take reasonable care not to cause injury to persons or "other" property*

2–40   Delete first sentence and substitute: In *Targett* v. *Torfaen Borough Council*,[28a] the Court of Appeal held that a local authority that had designed and built a council house was liable to a tenant who had been injured as a result of the negligent failure to provide a handrail or adequate lighting, notwithstanding the plaintiff's knowledge of the defects that had caused his injuries. The Court refused to accede to the defendant's argument that the effect of *Murphy* v. *Brentwood District Council* [1991] 1 A.C. 398 was that the local authority was not liable for injuries caused by patent defects. Both Leggatt L.J. (at p. 36a) and Sir Donald Nicholls V.-C. (at p. 37b–j) emphasised that the essential question was whether it was reasonable for a plaintiff to avoid a danger once he was aware of the same. On the facts of the case a weekly tenant was in no position to remedy the dangerous situation and the Council was therefore liable, although a deduction of 25 per cent. was appropriate for the plaintiff's contributory negligence in failing to look where he was going. In *Nitrigin Eireann Teoranta* v. *Inco Alloys Ltd.* [1992] 1 W.L.R. 498 May J. on the hearing of preliminary issues found (*a*) that no cause of action had arisen when a pipe supplied by specialist pipe-makers to a building owner cracked and was repaired but (*b*) that the pipe makers were liable for the losses caused by a subsequent explosion when the pipe cracked again a year later causing damage to the surrounding plant. His finding was based on the assumption that it was reasonable for the plaintiff not to discover (and thus repair) the cause of cracking when it first occurred.[28b] In the light of *Targett*, this finding appears correct. However the judge's further statement, *obiter* at p. 506, that even if the plaintiff ought reasonably to have diagnosed the cause of the cracking on the first occasion, this would not have affected the accrual of a cause of action on the second, is inconsistent with the reasoning in *Targett*.[28c]

NOTE 28a. [1992] 3 All E.R. 27; [1992] P.I.Q.R. P125.

NOTE 28b. See also McGee, "Back to Pirelli" (1992) 108 L.Q.R. 364 where this decision is discussed.

NOTE 28c. See also the decision of the Nova Scotia Court of Appeal in *A.C.A. Cooperative* v. *Associated Freezers* (1992) 93 D.L.R. 559. The Court found the defendant engineers liable to bailors for damage caused to goods left in a warehouse when the roof collapsed under snow-load as a result of the negligent design, by the engineers, of the roof. Although the owners and occupiers of the warehouse were also found to have been negligent for failing to correct the design defect, this negligence was not found to break the chain of causation. Similarly in *Pantalone* v. *Alaouie* (1989) 18 N.S.W.L.R. 119, Giles J. found engineers engaged by the owner of a building liable to the owner of an adjoining building which collapsed as a result of the engineer having failed to make known to his client the full extent and danger of undertaking excavations without taking proper precautions.

Add to NOTE 32: Similarly in *Canberra Formwork Pty. Ltd.* v. *Civil & Civic Ltd.* (1982) 41 A.C.T.R. 1, Blackburn C.J., in the Supreme Court of the Australian Capital Territory, found a site engineer employed by a building contractor liable for the death of a workman for failing to take reasonable steps to prevent the use of a dangerous formwork box on site. **2–41**

(d) *Save in special circumstances, a building professional will not owe a duty of care to prevent economic loss*

Add: Similarly in *Hiron* v. *Pynford South Ltd.*, 60 B.L.R. 78; (1992) 28 E.G. 112; [1992] C.I.L.L. 716, His Honour Judge Newey Q.C. found on a hearing of preliminary issues that engineers instructed by an insurance company to assess damage to an insured property did not owe a duty of care to the assured property owners not to cause them economic loss. He also found that the engineers did not owe a concurrent duty in tort to the insurance company. See further the supplement to note 64 to § 2–19, above. **2–46**

Add to NOTE 44: The plaintiff's appeal (which concerned the action against the land-owner alone) was dismissed and is reported at 60 B.L.R. 1.

Add to NOTE 50: Mr. Donald Keating Q.C. has questioned whether this case is still good law at (1992) 8 Const.L.J. 405, 406. **2–47**

2–48   Add to NOTE 54: In *Nitrigin Eireann Teoranta* v. *Inco Alloys Ltd.*
[1992] 1 W.L.R. 498, 505, May J. stated that it would be intellectually
dishonest to distinguish that case from *Junior Books* and did not do so.
The judge simply declined to apply it on the basis that it was unique and
depended in some (unspecified) way on *Hedley Byrne & Co. Ltd.* v.
Heller & Partners Ltd. [1964] A.C. 465.

Insert new paragraph after § 2–48:

2–48A   The tendency of the English Courts to adopt a restrictive approach in
deciding whether or not a particular set of facts fall into a "special"
category are well-illustrated by the decision of the Court of Appeal in
Preston v. *Torfaen Borough Council.*[54a] The plaintiffs were the first
purchasers from a local authority of a house which had been built on an
in-filled quarry. The defendants were the engineers who had carried out
the site investigation for the local authority. It was accepted, for the
purposes of a preliminary issue (1) that the defendants had held themselves out as experts to give specific advice for a specific purpose; (2) that
they must have known that the local authority would rely on that advice
as it in fact did; (3) that the local authority had power to sell the house;
and (4) that the defendants must have known that whoever occupied the
house at the time that the defects became manifest would inevitably
suffer economic loss as a result of any negligent advice. In the absence of
any form of negligent misstatement by the defendants to the plaintiffs,
the Court of Appeal found that the above facts were not sufficient to
ground liability in negligence. Sir Michael Fox pointed out that a builder
would not have been liable to the plaintiff and did not consider that there
was any reason for the defendants to be placed in any different position.
The only possible remedy for the plaintiffs would appear to have been
pursuant to the Defective Premises Act 1972: see §§2–17—2–18 above.
     NOTE 54a. [1993] C.I.L.L. 864.

2–50   Add: In *University of Regina* v. *Pettick*[61a] the Saskatchewan Court of
Appeal considered a claim by a university against defendant architects
and engineers for defects in a gymnasium which they had designed. The
Court categorised the claim as being one for economic losses and rejected
the claim against the architects on the grounds that they had fulfilled their
obligations by ensuring that reasonably competent engineers were
appointed. On the basis of the two-stage test in *Anns*,[61b] the Court found
the engineers to be liable. A proximate relationship was created as a
result of a call by the university for testing which the engineers undertook
to provide.[61c] It is unlikely that the case would now be decided the same
way in England.
     Add to NOTE 58: See also the decision of the Lin Beng Choon J. in the
Malaysian High Court in *Chin Sin Motor Works* v. *Arosa Development*

Sdn Bhd [1992] 1 M.L.J. 23 (architects employed by developer liable for negligent misstatements in certificates relied on by the plaintiff purchaser and financier).

NOTE 61a. (1992) 77 D.L.R. (4th) 615.

NOTE 61b. Which was held still to be good law in Canada: see further new § 2–36A, above.

NOTE 61c. See especially pp. 655–657 *per* Sherstobitoff J.A.

Add new paragraphs after § 2–53:

In Canada, the Supreme Court has now decided in *Edgeworth Con-* **2–53A** *struction* v. *N.D. Lea and Walji*,[69a] that a contractor which relied on tender documents prepared by engineers for the employer in order to put forward a price can sue the engineers for economic losses sustained as a result of negligent errors in such documents. This was so even though there was an express term in the contract between the employer and the contractor that any representations in the tender documents were furnished merely for information and did not amount to warranties. McLachlin J. (with whom five of the other six judges concurred) took the view that the errors amounted to negligent misrepresentations which the engineers knew would be likely to be relied on by the contractor and were in fact relied upon. The claim fell within the principle set out in *Hedley Byrne* and the subsequent decision of the Supreme Court of Canada in *Haig* v. *Bamford*.[69b] The judge considered the only real question to be whether the terms of the contract between the contractor and the employer negated the duty of care which would otherwise have been held to have arisen. It was held that the contract did not provide the engineers with protection (a) because it did not purport to do so and (b) because the engineers could have taken alternative measures to protect themselves by, for example, putting a disclaimer on its design documents. McLachlin J. did not consider that there were any policy considerations militating against the imposition of a duty of care: he pointed out that it made greater practical sense for the pre-tender engineering work to be done by one firm rather than have all tenderers checking such work.

The decision is consistent with the earlier case of *Auto Concrete Curb* **2–53B** *Ltd.* v. *South Nation River Conservation Authority*[69c] where the Ontario Court of Appeal held that an engineer was liable to a contractor for negligence in the pre-engineering stage of a tender process for a contract for dredging a river. The essential findings of fact upon which liability was founded were (*a*) that two alternative methods of performing the contract would have been within the contemplation of a reasonably competent engineer who was preparing tender documents; (*b*) that a reasonably competent engineer would have made inquiries of statutory authorities having jurisdiction in relation to the project and included relevant information in the tender documents (such inquiries would have revealed the need for additional permits for one of the methods); (c) that the engineer knew or ought to have known that the contractor and other bidders would rely on the information contained in the tender documents and the failure to include relevant information constituted a negligent misrepresentation; (d) that the need to obtain permits was not one that was made known or was reasonably foreseeable from the bid documents; and (e) that it was not reasonable to expect the contractor within a two-week period for tender to canvass and make enquiries when the engineer had had some four months to make appropriate enquiries.

NOTE 69a. [1993] 8 W.W.R 129 overturning the previous decision of the Court of Appeal of British Columbia reported at (1991) 54 Build.L.R. 16.

NOTE 69b. [1977] 1 S.C.R. 466.

NOTE 69c. (1992) 89 D.L.R. (4th) 393.

The certificate cases

2–57   Add: In England, it may be possible to circumvent the restrictions imposed by the Court of Appeal's decision by alleging alternative causes of action providing, of course, the appropriate factual basis exists. In *John Mowlem* v. *Eagle Star*,[83a] His Honour Judge Loyd Q.C. refused to strike out a claim by a contractor against an architect for unlawful interference with contract and conspiracy. The architect was named as such in the management contract between the contractor and the developer (which subsequently became insolvent). The contractor alleged (1) that it was an implied term of the management contract that the developer would not interfere or obstruct the architect in relation to the issue of certificates under the contract; and (2) that the architect had failed to act independently and had deliberately misapplied the contract with the intention of depriving the contractor of sums to which it was entitled.

NOTE 83a. 62 B.L.R. 126.

2–58   Add to NOTE 85: *Edgeworth Construction* v. *N.D. Lea and Walji* has now been reversed by the Supreme Court of Canada. See further § 2–53A, above and § 2–59A, below.

Importance of contractual terms

Add new paragraphs after § 2–59:

2–59A   The Courts in Canada have recognised the importance of examining contractual terms in deciding whether tortious liability should be imposed. In *Edgeworth Construction* v. *N.D. Lea and Walji*[87a] the

Supreme Court considered that the existence and precise terms of a contract between an employer and a contractor did not prevent a claim by the contractor against the employer's engineers for alleged negligent misstatements made in the tender documents. The Court found that the contract did not, on a proper construction provide protection to the engineers and pointed out that the engineers could themselves have obtained such protection by an appropriate disclaimer on the tender documents.[87b]

It appears that in Canada it is or may be important for a plaintiff to be able to show that it has acted on statements which have been made to it so as to establish a cause of action. In the earlier case of *British Columbia Hydro & Power Authority* v. *N.D. Lea & Associates*[87c] Newbury J. dismissed a claim for economic loss against the same engineers by a statutory authority responsible for the construction of a dam. The authority was obliged to construct a new highway in order to replace one which would be flooded when the dam was full. Rather than itself constructing the highway, the authority agreed with the Ministry of Highways that the authority should pay for the highway but that the ministry should organise the design and construction. The ministry engaged the defendant engineers to design the highway. When heavy rain caused a culvert on the highway to be washed away, the authority considered itself bound to pay for a replacement bridge pursuant to the agreement between the ministry and the authority. The Judge did not consider the agreement to have this effect. However, even if it had, he considered that the defendants were not directly liable in tort to the authority. Having conducted a sweeping review of the authorities and policy issues he stated: **2–59B**

> "In the final analysis, the policy issues are almost evenly balanced. On one hand, there is negligence on the part of the defendant, a professional engineering firm which must be expected to carry insurance, and which, if recovery were denied, would effectively evade liability by virtue of a contractual provision of which it was not even aware. This is a result that rankles, even bearing in mind La Forest J.'s observations[87d] regarding the irrelevance of 'moral fault' in cases of this kind. Recovery would likely not open the door to indeterminate liability. On the other hand, if recovery were allowed, the court would effectively be creating rights akin to or even superior to, assignment or subrogation rights that were not negotiated or may have been rejected by two sophisticated parties at the time they made their agreement. In my opinion, the former choice is the lesser of two evils. It is supported by the authorities and does not operate to circumvent the law relating to contract and indemnity. It provides

certainty and predictability and encourages parties to act in a commercially reasonable manner. A finding of liability would go further than what is suggested by any of the judgments in *Jervis Crown* or any previous case."

NOTE 87a. (1993) 8 W.W.R. 129.

NOTE 87b. See further new § 2–53A, above.

NOTE 87c. (1992) 69 B.C.L.R. (2d) 309.

NOTE 87d. In *Canadian National Railway Co.* v. *Norsk Pacific Steamship Co.* (1992) 137 N.R. 241: see new § 2–36A, above.

(iii) The Standard of Care and Skill

(a) *The ordinary competent and skilled practitioner*

2–61   Add new NOTE 92a after the first sentence: In *Larche* v. *Ontario* (1990) 75 D.L.R. (4th) 377, the Ontario Court of Appeal upheld the trial judge's rejection of a claim that architects were liable to a patient at a psychiatric hospital who was injured when he fell from the roof as a result of alleged negligence in the design of a railing. The Court (at p. 380) upheld the judge's finding that "what was designed was reasonable and represented the discharge of the architects' duty to design a barrier which 'met an acceptable security standard in the particular location it was constructed at this type of psychiatric facility.' " See further Chap. 6, § 6–133, below.

Add to NOTE 1: In *Pullen* v. *Gutteridge* [1993] 1 V.R. 27 at p. 52, the Court of Appeal of Victoria found engineers who had designed a swimming pool complex negligent for not warning about the risks of their foundation design and for having failed to give advice as to possible alternatives.

(d) *Special steps and warranty of reasonable fitness*

2–71   Add to NOTE 53: In *B.C. Rail Ltd.* v. *Canadian Pacific Consulting Services Ltd.* (1990) 47 B.C.L.R. 49 the British Columbia Court of Appeal found there to be an implied warranty of fitness for purpose in a contract where the defendant engineers had agreed to design and install an overhead contact system for a railway line. The warranty was found to be both reasonable and necessary on a proper construction of the contract.

2.—LIABILITY FOR BREACH OF DUTY

(ii) Errors in Design

2–85   The Court of Appeal of Victoria followed *City of Brantford* in *Pullen* v. *Gutteridge*,[2a] in finding that engineers who had designed a swimming pool complex were negligent in not having warned the employer about the risks involved in their design and for not having suggested possible alternatives. The complex was constructed in an area with complex ground conditions and the Court also found the engineers to be liable for not having taken into account experience at another, relatively nearby, site where long-term settlements had been experienced. It was held that either the engineers should have carried out further investigations to see whether similar settlements were likely or the complex should have been designed on the assumption that such settlements would be experienced.[2b]

NOTE 2a. [1993] 1 V.R. 27.

NOTE 2b. *Ibid.* at p. 48.

(iii) Providing a Misleading Estimate

Add to NOTE 20: See also the South-African case of *Wilkens Nel* **2–89** *Argitekte* v. *Stephenson* [1987] 2 S.A.L.R. 628 in which the Orange Free State Provincial Court of Appeal held that architects, who accepted instructions containing a specific requirement that the final cost of the project was in no circumstances to exceed the estimated cost of R100,000, were not entitled to fees for drawing up plans when it became clear that the cost of the project built in accordance with those plans would be substantially higher than the estimated cost.

(iv) Errors in Preparation of Bills of Quantities

Add to NOTE 32: For discussion of the Canadian cases where claims by **2–93** contractors against engineers who prepared tender documents have been allowed, see §2–53A above.

(viii) Failure to Administer Building Contract Properly

Add after NOTE 49: The difficulties which can face an architect when **2–97** faced with a recalcitrant contractor are shown by *West Faulkner Associates* v. *London Borough of Newham.*[49a] The defendant architects were engaged by a local authority to act as architect in respect of the refurbishment of a large number of flats which was being carried out by the contractor pursuant to JCT Standard Form of building contract, 1963 edition, 1977 revision. As a result of the contractor's inability properly to programme and supervise the works, the programme time was substantially exceeded. Although His Honour Judge Newey Q.C. had sympathy for the architects, he found them to have been negligent in failing to serve a notice under clause 25(1)(b) of the contract stating that the contractor was failing to proceed regularly and diligently with the works which would have led to the local authority being able to terminate the contractor's employment if the latter's performance had not improved. The Judge said,[49b]

> "The Architects were without authoritative guidance as to the meaning of 'regularly and diligently.' They thought that provided [the contractor] had men and materials on site and were doing some work within the contractual period they were proceeding regularly and diligently. They did not seek to confirm this belief by consulting more experienced Architects than themselves, taking legal advice or urging the Council to take legal advice and communicate it to them . . .
>
> I think that if [the contractor's] failures had been less glaringly obvious the Architects might have been justified in not serving a notice upon them—at least until they had obtained reliable guidance. Since however, [the contractor's] failures were so very extreme, I think that the Architects should have realised that [the contractor] could not possibly be proceeding regularly and diligently and have given a notice to them. I feel sure that the ordinary competent Architect would have taken that course . . .. This was not a marginal case."

In *Corfield* v. *Grant*[49c] His Honour Judge Bowsher Q.C. found an architect to be in breach of duty by reason of his failure properly to control a building project. The judge was particularly critical of the architect's failure to appoint and direct a suitably skilled and experienced assistant in a situation where the architect knew that speed was of the essence and it was necessary to organise a large number of matters at the same time. The judge found the architect to be responsible for the resultant "inadequately controlled muddle."

NOTE 49a. (1992) 31 Con. L.R. 105.
NOTE 49b. *Ibid.* at p. 140.
NOTE 49c. (1992) 29 Con. L.R. 58.

(ix) Inadequate Supervision

2–98   Add to NOTE 50: The obligations imposed on an architect by his duty to supervise were briefly considered in *Corfield* v. *Grant* (1992) 29 Con.L.R. 58 where His Honour Judge Bowsher Q.C. stated:

> "What is adequate by way of supervision and other work is not in the end to be tested by the number of hours worked on site or elsewhere, but by asking whether it was enough. At some stages of some jobs exclusive attention may be required to the job in question (either in the office or on site): at other stages of the same job, or during most of the duration of other jobs, it will be quite sufficient to

give attention to the job only from time to time. The proof of the pudding is in the eating. Was the attention given enough for this particular job?"

Unfortunately the report does not make it clear whether the judge was discussing a contract where the architect was, in truth, obliged to supervise or whether he merely had an obligation of inspection. The passage set out above is unexceptionable insofar as it states that a reasonably competent architect will realise that he needs to vary his input according to the nature of the job for which he is retained and the stage such a job has reached. Nevertheless insofar as the judge suggests that an architect's performance should be judged by the result achieved, it is submitted that the passage goes too far. An architect's duty is to exercise reasonable skill and care in seeking to achieve a particular result not to guarantee that a particular result will be achieved.

In *Rowlands* v. *Collow* [1992] 1 N.Z.L.R. 178, 197 Thomas J. drew a distinction between an engineer's obligation to "supervise" a building contract which involved "detailed and continuous direction" and an obligation to provide observation by way of oversight which required an engineer to carry out such inspections as were necessary to confirm that a design was being interpreted correctly and to ascertain that the works were being carried out in accordance with the contract documents. The judge held that the engineer in an informal contract concerning the provision of a driveway was only under the latter obligation but was nonetheless in breach of the same.

Add to NOTE 74: See also *Canberra Formwork Pty. Ltd.* v. *Civil &* **2–102** *Civic Ltd.* (1982) 41 A.C.T.R. 1, where the Supreme Court of the Australian Capital Territory found a site engineer liable to a formwork employee who was killed during a concrete pour. The site engineer was held to be negligent in failing to take reasonable steps to prevent the use of a dangerous formwork box, such as reporting the circumstances fully to the site manager, even though the engineer had no power to stop work on site.

(x) Incorrect Certification

Add to NOTE 93: In *Rowlands* v. *Collow* [1992] 1 N.Z.L.R. 178, 200 **2–106** Thomas J. held that an engineer who certified the value of work done in an informal contract for the provision of a driveway accepted an obligation to inspect and assess the value of the work which had, in fact, been completed.

Add new heading:

(xii) Inadequate Investigation of Defects

2–108A   It may sometimes be the case that a primary cause of action will be statute-barred against designers but a plaintiff will wish to allege that he should nonetheless be entitled to recover. This interesting question arose in *Pullen* v. *Gutteridge*,[97a] where the Court of Appeal of Victoria considered two actions against a firm of engineers. In the first action, the plaintiff alleged that the engineers had negligently designed a swimming pool complex. The engineers claimed that this action was statute-barred both in contract and in tort. The plaintiff accordingly commenced a second action alleging (1) that the engineers had failed to investigate defects properly during the limitation period; (2) that as a result of their negligence, the plaintiff had lost the opportunity of obtaining competent advice from other sources; and (3) that if they had obtained such advice, proceedings would have been commenced during the limitation period. The Court of Appeal found that the engineers were liable in the first action,[97b] and that the defence of limitation failed but nonetheless went on to consider the second action in case they were wrong in respect of their treatment of the first action. Its conclusion was expressed as follows[97c]:

> "Had the respondent acted with reasonable care when asked to investigate and report to the appellant, its investigations would have had two consequences. In the first place, it would have come to realise, or at the very least to entertain a strong suspicion, that its own design of the sub-structure was seriously deficient and that the deficiency was responsible for many of the defects that had emerged and were emerging. In the second place, it would have communicated this realisation or suspicion to its client."

NOTE 97a. [1993] 1 V.R. 27.
NOTE 97b. See supplement to § 2–85 above.
NOTE 97c. *Ibid.* at p. 86.

3.—DAMAGES

(i) Remoteness

(a) *Causation*

Intervening act of plaintiff or third party

2–112   Add at the end of the paragraph: In *Targett* v. *Torfaen Borough Council*[21a] the Court of Appeal emphasised that the essential question, in deciding whether a tortfeasor was liable for personal injuries caused by a

defect of which the plaintiff had knowledge, was whether it was reasonable for the plaintiff to avoid the danger given the knowledge. See further
the supplement to § 2–40, above.

NOTE 21a. [1992] 3 All E.R. 27; [1992] P.I.Q.R. P125.

(iii) Heads of Damage

Add new paragraph and sub-heading:

(aa) *Diminution in value*

In certain cases it may be appropriate to award the diminution in value   **2–125A**
of land or property rather than the cost of repairing the same. In
Pantalone v. *Alaouie*[59a] an engineer was found to be liable for the collapse
of a building as a result of his negligence in failing to make clear to the
owner of the adjoining property the precautions that would be required
before undertaking excavations. Giles J. considered [59b] that the essential
question was whether it was reasonable to rebuild the building "judged in
part by the advantages [to the plaintiffs] of rebuilding in relation to the
additional cost to the defendants over the diminution in value." Having
decided, on the facts, that it would not be reasonable he therefore
awarded diminution in value plus conveyancing costs (to reflect the fact
that it was likely that the site would be sold and a replacement property
purchased).

NOTE 59a. (1989) 18 N.S.W.L.R. 119.
NOTE 59b. At p. 138.

(c) *Excess expenditure*

A recent example of the recovery of such expenditure is shown by the   **2–127**
West Faulkner Associates v. *London Borough of Newham.*[63a] His Honour
Judge Newey Q.C. held that as a result of the architect's negligent failure
to service a notice under the building contract stating that the contractor
was not proceeding regularly and diligently with the works, the employer
lost the opportunity to be placed in a favourable contractual situation
with regard to the contractor. As a result the employer was entitled to
recover the additional costs charged by new, replacement, contractors,
professional fees and certain other consequential losses which should not
have been incurred.

NOTE 63c. (1993) 9 Const. L.J. 232 (for facts see § 2–97 above).

(h) *Inconvenience*

Add new NOTE 76a: after the penultimate sentence. In *Rowlands* v.   **2–132**
Collow [1992] 1 N.Z.L.R. 178, 205–209, Thomas J. in the High Court of
New Zealand refused to follow *Hayes* v. *Dodd* and instead found that
damages for mental distress should be awarded whenever they were in

the contemplation of the parties at the time a contract was made. He made an award of $18,000NZ to three plaintiffs who had had to use an inconvenient driveway for access to their properties as a result of an engineer's failure to design the same competently.

Add to NOTE 77: K. Franklin has carried out a further review of the recent authorities in the light of *Watts* v. *Morrow* in (1992) 8 Const.L.J. 318.

(v) Shared Responsibility

2–134 Add to NOTE 85: *Oxford University Press* v. *John Stedman Design Group* is now reported at 34 Con. L.R. 1.

CHAPTER 3

SURVEYORS

1.—GENERAL

Surveyors as expert witnesses

Add NOTE 18A: Guidance as to the duties and responsibilities of expert **3–06** witnesses in civil cases has been given by the Court of Appeal in *National Justice Compania Naviera S.A.* v. *Prudential Assurance Co. Ltd.* [1993] 2 Lloyd's Rep. 68.

(i) Bases of Liability

Add: In *Hiron* v. *Pynford South Ltd.* (1992) 2 E.G.L.R. 138, the **3–07** Official Referee, Judge Newey Q.C., held that the fourth defendant firm of building surveyors did not owe a duty of care to the first plaintiffs since they had entered into an express contract whereby a duty in tort to take care would merely have duplicated an implied term in the contract. To impose such a duty would not have been just and reasonable since the only probable result would have been to give the first plaintiffs a longer period in which to sue them. If that had been the intention of the parties they could have provided for it in the contract. The judge commented that the conclusion would probably have been different if the contractual and tortious duties had not precisely coincided (*ibid.* at p. 141H).

Add to NOTE 31: In *Horbury* v. *Craig Hall & Rutley* (1991) 7 P.N. 206 **3–08** the plaintiff purchased a property in November 1980 relying on the defendant's survey report. In March 1984 the plaintiff was told by a builder that certain chimney breasts were unsupported and dangerous and she paid £132 for repair work. In July 1985 the plaintiff discovered dry rot in the floors. In February 1988 the plaintiff issued a writ claiming damages in tort for the consequences of a negligent survey. The judge held that the defendants had been negligent in failing to observe the unsupported flues, and in failing to warn the plaintiff of the risk of rot affecting the floors. However the plaintiff's claim was statute-barred. The three-year discoverability period under the Limitation Act 1980, s.14A ran from the date when the plaintiff first had knowledge of the material facts concerning the damage in respect of which damages were claimed. The damage was the purchase of the property in November 1980 in reliance on a negligent survey report. The plaintiff acquired the relevant knowledge in March 1984 when she was told of the unsupported flues. This was more than three years before the writ was issued. The judge held that the facts known in March 1984 were such as to meet the requirements of section 14A(7).

For a discussion on the effect of the Latent Damage Act 1986 on surveyors reports and valuations, see T. Dugdale, "Latent Damage: The Application of the Discoverability Principle to Survey Reports" (1991) 7 P.N. 193.

Insert new paragraphs after § 3–09:

Contributory negligence

3–09A   A negligent surveyor has the same right as any other defendant to defend an action against him by alleging that the plaintiff was negligent, and that such negligence caused, or contributed to, any loss proved. Contributory negligence does not involve breach of duty owed by a plaintiff to a defendant, but the failure by the plaintiff to use reasonable care to protect its own interests. This topic is discussed in Chap. 1, § 1–82. However, a valuer personally or vicariously liable to the plaintiff for deceit is not entitled, either at common law or by reason of sections 1(1) and 4 of the Law Reform (Contributory Negligence) Act 1945, to plead by way of defence that the plaintiff was guilty of contributory negligence. See *Alliance & Leicester Building Society and others* v. *Edgestop Ltd. and others* [1993] 1 W.L.R. 1462. The plaintiffs were the victims of a large scale mortgage fraud, one of the actors being a valuer, Mr. Lancaster, at the time an employee of Hamptons Residential, and subsequently convicted of offences of dishonesty involving the material valuations. Hamptons applied to amend their defence to allege that the plaintiffs were guilty of contributory negligence in failing to discover that Mr. Lancaster was acting outside the scope of his employment, in failing to detect the dishonest nature of the applications for a mortgage, and in failing to act as a prudent lender in respect of the processing of the mortgage applications. Mummery J. held that prior to the 1945 Act, the contributory negligence of a plaintiff suing in deceit could not be pleaded as a defence (p. 1474F) and that the position had not been changed by the 1945 Act (p. 1477D).

In a decision given on December 21, 1993 (unreported) in the same **3–09B** case, Mummery J. concluded that whilst Mr. Lancaster had not been acting within the scope of his actual authority in valuing the properties, he had been acting within his ostensible authority, that the plaintiffs had not had notice of his want of authority when they relied upon the valuations and that Hamptons were, therefore, vicariously liable for Mr. Lancaster's deceit.

For a discussion of contributory negligence and imprudent lending see § 3–103A.

Defective Premises Act 1972

Since January 1, 1974, section 1 of the Defective Premises Act 1972 has **3–09C** imposed on a person taking on work for or in connection with the provision of a dwelling a duty to see that the work which he takes on is done in a workmanlike, or as the case may be, professional manner, with proper materials and so that as regards that work the dwelling will be fit for habitation when completed. The duty is owed to the person to whose order the dwelling is provided and to every person who acquires an interest in the dwelling. Defective Premises Act 1972, s.1(1). A surveyor carrying out a survey or valuation of a dwelling would not ordinarily be regarded as "taking on work in connection with the provision of a dwelling" and so it is submitted has no liability in respect of such work under this Act. See further analysis in Holyoak & Allen, *Civil Liability for Defective Premises* (1982), Chapter 4 and M. F. James, "The Defective Premises Act and 'Fitness for Habitation' " (1993) 9 P.N. 144.

Insert new paragraphs after § 3–10:

Liability in respect of statements about property matters

The Property Misdescriptions Act 1991 provides that where a statement **3–10A** that is false or misleading to a material degree is made about property matters in the course of estate agency business, the person by whom the business is carried on shall be guilty of an offence: sections 1(1) and (5). The commission of an offence under this Act does not of itself render any associated contract void or unenforceable: section 1(4). Limitation periods for the commencement of a prosecution under the Act are three years from the date of the commission of the offence, or one year from the date of discovery of the offence by the prosecutor: section 5(1). The Act received the Royal Assent on June 27, 1991 and came into force on that date. The Property Misdescriptions (Specified Matters) Order was made on November 11, 1992, and came into force on April 4, 1993. The Schedule to the Order sets out the specified matters for the purposes of section 1(1). For commentary on this Act, see D. W. Oughton, "The Property Misdescriptions Act 1991" (1992) 8 P.N. 59 and G. Stephenson, "The Regulation of Estate Agency" (1992) 8 P.N. 2.

Liability in connection with a contravention of section 3 of the Financial Services Act 1986

3–10B   Valuers have a potential liability under this part of the Financial Services Act: F.S.A. 1986: see s.6. This is discussed in Chap. 1, § 1–139, and see *S.I.B.* v. *Pantell* [1992] 3 W.L.R. 896 for a case involving solicitors held at first instance liable under this legislation to repay investors, discussed at Chap. 1, § 1–140.

Liability under the ombudsman scheme

3–10C   An existing borrower from a building society, who, when seeking a further advance relies to his detriment on a negligent valuation or survey prepared by a surveyor employed by the building society, may be able to invoke the ombudsman procedure as an inexpensive alternative to litigation. Section 83(1) of the Building Societies Act 1986 confers on an individual the right as against a building society to have any complaint concerning action taken by the society in relation to certain matters investigated under a scheme recognised by the Building Societies Commission. On June 5, 1987 a building societies ombudsman scheme was recognised by the Commission. The ombudsman's duties include the obligation to investigate any complaint received by him from an individual if:

(*a*) The complaint relates to action taken in the United Kingdom by a building society;

(*b*) in relation to the grant or refusal to grant a borrowing member other or further advances secured on the same or different land provided that the grounds of complaint are that;

(*c*) the action complained of constitutes in relation to the complainant, in the case of a participating society, a breach of its obligations under the Building Societies Act 1986, its rules or any other contract, or unfair treatment or maladministration. See clauses 14, 17 and 18 of the scheme.

3–10D   Schedule 12 of the Act omitted any reference to surveys and valuations of land, therefore the only relevant matter of complaint is that part of paragraph 3 of Part II to Schedule 12 of the Act which refers to the grant or refusal to grant further advances to a borrowing member. The complainant must therefore have been an existing borrower at the time of the grant or refusal. Further, because the complaint must be about the acts or omissions of the society, the ombudsman has no jurisdiction to investigate complaints relating to valuations made by a non-employee surveyor. In *Halifax Building Society* v. *Edell* [1992] Ch. 436 Morritt J. held that the preparation, by surveyors directly employed by the plaintiff societies, of basic valuations, house-buyers reports and valuations, and structural surveys, in connection with applications for further advances by the second to ninth defendants, were all part of the society's process of administration. If negligently prepared, such work could amount to maladministration within Schedule 12 to the 1986 Act, and that accordingly, the ombudsman had jurisdiction to investigate and determine the borrower's complaints. The ombudsman scheme is dealt with more fully in Wurtzburg and Mills, *Building Society Law* (looseleaf, Stevens & Sons), Chap. 15.

(ii) Duties to Client

(a) *Contractual duties*

Add: It is submitted that a valuer is not under an implied duty to **3–12** proffer unsought advice on the wisdom of entering into a property transaction in which he has been retained for a clearly defined and limited purpose. See the reasoning in *Clark Boyce* v. *Mouat* [1993] 3 W.L.R. 1021, a solicitor's negligence case, considered at § 4–73A.

Add to NOTE 43: *Summers* v. *Congreve Horner & Co.* is now reported at [1991] 2 E.G.L.R. 139.

Guidance notes

NOTE 68. *Hacker* v. *Thomas Deal & Co.* is now reported at [1991] 2 **3–17** E.G.L.R. 161.

Add to NOTE 70: In *P.K. Finians International (U.K.) Ltd.* v. *Andrew Downs & Co. Ltd.* [1992] 1 E.G.L.R. 172 an allegation that the defendant valuer should not have made oral enquiries of the planning authorities was held unsustainable in view of the terms of guidance note 6 of the R.I.C.S. *Guidance Notes of the Valuation of Assets*. The deputy judge also commented, *ibid.* at p. 174K, that: "these guidance notes are not to be regarded as a statute . . . mere failure to comply with the guidance notes does not constitute negligence."

Add: In *European Partners in Capital (EPIC) Holdings B.V.* v. **3–18** *Goddard & Smith* [1992] 2 E.G.L.R. 155 the Court of Appeal held: "Issues of professional opinion, which must be chosen between if liability in negligence is to be established, will not as a general rule be issues suitable to be resolved on a summary judgment application." Scott L.J. at p. 157E.

Effect of Unfair Contract Terms Act 1977

3–20 Add NOTE 77a: For discussions of this Act and the case of *Stewart Gill Ltd.* v. *Horatio Myer & Co. Ltd.* [1992] 2 All E.R. 257, see Peel, "Making More Use of the Unfair Contract Terms Act 1977" (1993) 56 M.L.R. 98, and Brown and Chandler, "Unreasonableness and the Unfair Contract Terms Act" (1993) 109 L.Q.R. 41.

Building societies

3–21 Add: A report from an employee of a building society may in certain circumstances render the society liable to an investigation by the building societies ombudsman: see § 3–10C, above.

(iii) Duties to Third Parties

Add new paragraph after § 3–28:

3–28A The impact of *Murphy* v. *Brentwood District Council* [1991] 1 A.C. 398 is discussed at § 1–39. Where the loss suffered is properly characterised as pure economic loss, the tort of negligence will generally not impose liability. In such circumstances the absence of a contractual relationship will be fatal to recovery. However, where the relationship between the parties is particularly close, the courts will impose a duty, including a duty to prevent pure economic loss. See, for example, *Smith* v. *Eric S. Bush* [1990] 1 A.C. 831, discussed at § 3–37, and *White* v. *Jones* [1993] 3 W.L.R. 730, discussed at § 4–25 (and see the discussion of *Ross* v. *Caunters* [1980] Ch. 297, at § 4–16). An attempt to impose a similarly close relationship was made in *Preston* v. *Torfaen Borough Council and another* [1993] E.G.C.S. 137. The plaintiff purchased a house on an estate built by the defendant council over, allegedly, an infilled quarry. The defendant engineers had provided the council with a report on soil conditions and, it was alleged, negligently failed to identify the nature of the site. The action against the council was abandoned after the decision in *Murphy*, that against the engineers was pursued to the Court of Appeal on a preliminary issue as to whether the engineers owed a duty of care to the plaintiff. The Court of Appeal held that no duty was owed. The engineers were no more proximate to the plaintiff than the builders, who could not be sued by reason of *Murphy*. The duty owed by the engineers to the council could not be extended to the plaintiff, as a potential purchaser he was an unidentified member of a class, and further, a class that would not ask to see the report before purchase. These principles will apply to reports prepared in similar circumstances by surveyors. See further commentary at § 2–48A.

(c) *Duty of mortgagee's valuer to purchaser*

Insert new paragraph after § 3–41:

An unintended consequence of the decision in *Smith* v. *Eric S. Bush* is **3–41A** that a valuer may be exposed to double jeopardy in respect of the same negligent valuation. In factual circumstances similar to those which obtained in *Smith* v. *Eric S. Bush* the valuer will owe a contractual duty to the lender, and a duty of care at common law to the borrower. An overvaluation caused by a negligent failure to observe defects may result in the borrower suing the valuer. Having recovered damages the borrower may not carry out repairs but instead may dissipate the fruits of the action. If there is a subsequent default by the borrower, the lender has a right to claim its loss from the valuer. The valuer cannot defeat such a claim on the basis that it has already met the claim by the borrower. The parties were different, the cause of action was different and the measure of damage was different. To reduce the risk of such a situation arising a potentially negligent valuer might wish to involve the lender at an appropriate stage in any action brought by the borrower.

(iv) The Standard of Care and Skill

(b) *General practice and knowledge as evidence of the standard*

Add to NOTE 68: See also *Mount Banking Corporation Ltd.* v. *Brian* **3–44** *Cooper & Co.* [1992] 2 E.G.L.R. 142, 144 where dicta to the same effect appears. The deputy judge at p. 145K considered the proper approach to be: "assess here whether [the valuer's] approach was proper and what a competent approach could properly have resulted in. If [the valuer's] end result was within a modest margin of that figure, then he is not to be adjudged negligent."

(d) *Onus of proof*

Add new NOTE 4a at end of the paragraph: This paragraph was cited **3–52** with approval in *Macey* v. *Debenham, Tewson & Chinnocks* [1993] 1 E.G.L.R. 149, 151M.

(v) Limitation of Liability

NOTE 36. *Beaton* v. *Nationwide Building Society* is now reported at **3–63** [1991] 2 E.G.L.R. 145.

NOTE 38. *Henley* v. *Cloke & Sons* is now reported at [1991] 2 E.G.L.R. **3–64** 141.

Scotland

3–65   Add to NOTE 41: Contrast with *Melrose* v. *Davidson & Robertson*, 1992
S.L.T. 395 where Lord Morton of Shuna construed an exclusion clause as
a term of the contract between the purchasers and the building society,
thereby allowing section 16 of the Unfair Contract Terms Act 1977 to
exclude the effect of the clause. Section 68 of the Law Reform (Miscellaneous Provisions) (Scotland) Act 1990 did not apply to the case. On
a reclaiming motion, the First Division of the Inner House declined to
interfere with the findings of Lord Morton of Shuna, see 1993 S.L.T. 611.

Add to text at end of paragraph: Section 68 of the Law Reform
(Miscellaneous Provisions) (Scotland) Act 1990, amended Part II of the
Unfair Contract Terms Act 1977 to bring non-contractual notices within
the statutory restrictions. Scots law was thereby made equivalent to
English law after *Smith* v. *Eric S. Bush*, as discussed in § 3–64, above.
The amendments were not retrospective and will only apply to liability
for any loss and damage suffered after April 1, 1991 when the section
came into force. See section 68(6) and Law Reform (Miscellaneous
Provisions) (Scotland) Act 1990 (Commencement No. 3) Order 1991 (S.I.
1991 No. 330).

(vi) Mutual Valuer

3–67   Add to NOTE 49: Where valuers appointed by each party are unable to
agree a valuation because of differences as to the proper approach, the
court may be prepared to make declarations as to the factors to be taken
into account. See *Little Hayes Nursing Home Ltd.* v. *Marshall* [1993]
E.G.C.S. 32 (valuation of property on the exercise of an option), and
Mid Kent Water plc v. *Batchelor and others* [1993] E.G.C.S. 103.

2.—LIABILITY FOR BREACH OF DUTY

(iii) Failing to Inspect Properly

(b) *Failing to uncover and open up*

3–79   NOTE 83. *Hacker* v. *Thomas Deal & Co.* is now reported at [1991] 2
E.G.L.R. 161.

3–80   NOTE 90. *Hacker* v. *Thomas Deal & Co.* is now reported at [1991] 2
E.G.L.R. 161.

(c) *Failing to observe*

Dry rot and woodworm

3–85   NOTES 8, 12 and 15. *Hacker* v. *Thomas Deal & Co.* is now reported at
[1991] 2 E.G.L.R. 161.

NOTE 15. Add to cases where surveyors were held not liable: *Kerridge* v. *James Abbott & Partners* [1992] 2 E.G.L.R. 162.

Defects in roof

Add to NOTE 19: See also *Heatley* v. *William H. Brown Ltd.* [1992] 1 **3–86** E.G.L.R. 289 where the surveyor retained to provide a structural survey was unable to gain access to the roof voids and discussed with the plaintiffs the absence of such access. Despite such conversation, and the incorporation into the retainer of the defendants' written conditions of engagement which included reference to the limitations in a report where parts of the property were unexposed or inaccessible, the defendants were held to have provided a negligent report. A subsequent inspection, after the plaintiffs had purchased the property and provided access to the roof voids was also held to have been negligent.

(e) *Failing to recognise*

Add: In *Bryan Peach* v. *Iain G. Chalmers & Co.* (1992) S.C.L.R. 423; **3–93** [1992] 2 E.G.L.R. 135, Outer House, Lord Caplan, a surveyor preparing a valuation and report misunderstood and misdescribed the construction of the house, which was of the Dorran-type construction. The property was valued as if it were of traditional construction. There was a risk, never explained to the purchasers, that the bolts holding together the pre-cast concrete panels could corrode, requiring expensive repairs. As a consequence the property could prove difficult to sell, as lending institutions would be reluctant to lend on the security of the same. The pursuers overpaid by £9,000 and this sum with varied rate simple interest was awarded.

(iv) Failing to Make Sufficient Inquiries

Add NOTE 52a on line 7 after the reference to hearsay information: It is **3–96** not necessary for evidence of comparable properties to be strictly proved where the evidence establishes that competent valuers make valuations on the basis of market intelligence which is hearsay. In *Banque Bruxelles Lambert S.A.* v. *Lewis & Tucker Ltd. and others (No. 1)*, February 26, 1993 (unreported), Phillips J. distinguished *English Exporters (London) Ltd.* v. *Eldonwall Ltd.* [1973] 1 Ch. 415, which itself was approved by the Court of Appeal in *Rogers* v. *Rosedimond Investments* [1978] 247 E.G. 467. Phillips J. concluded:

"One would of course normally expect the actual value of a property *i.e.* the value that it would actually realise on the market, to tally with the opinion of competent valuers as to its value. But the questions what is the actual value and what opinion would a competent valuer form of the actual value are two different questions and it is the latter with which I am concerned. *English Exporters* and *Rogers* v. *Rosedimond* were concerned with the former question and I do not consider that the principles pronounced in those cases are applicable in this."

The methodology discussed by Phillips J. was considered in *Zubaida* v. *Hargreaves* [1993] 43 E.G. 111. It was held that the defendant valuer, appointed as an independent expert to determine the rent of a restaurant on a rent review, acted in accordance with a practice accepted as proper by competent, respected, and professional opinion, in using as comparables rents of similar shop units.

(v) Failing to Make a Proper Appraisal

3–97   Add to NOTE 56. For an example, see *Macey* v. *Debenham, Tewson & Chinnocks* [1993] 1 E.G.L.R. 149 where the plaintiff, a solicitor, retained the defendant valuers to advise in respect of the proposed purchase for investment of certain freehold property. The advice given was to purchase the property, such advice included an analysis of yields. The plaintiff's claim failed, he having failed to prove that the valuers report, and the calculations and deductions on which it was based, were such as could not have been arrived at if he had shown reasonable skill and care.

Add to NOTE 57. For a case where, applying the dicta of Watkins J. in *Singer & Friedlander Ltd.* v. *John D. Wood & Co.* (1977) 243 E.G. 212, the valuation was considered to be within the bracket into which any proper valuation should have fallen, see *Muldoon* v. *Mays of Lilliput Ltd.* [1993] 1 E.G.L.R. 43. In *Private Bank & Trust Co. Ltd* v. *S. (U.K.) Ltd.* [1993] 1 E.G.L.R. 144 the court concluded that on the evidence the defendant's valuations lay within a permissible margin of error of 15 per cent. either side of his bracket. In *Banque Bruxelles Lambert S.A.* v. *Lewis & Tucker Ltd. and others,* December 21, 1993 (unreported), the evidence before Phillips J. was that when valuations are based on comparables, one competent valuation may differ from another by as much as 20 per cent. See judgment, p. 46.

Add new paragraph after § 3–97:

3–97A   The fact that a valuer makes a material and negligent error in reaching his figure will not establish liability where the total valuation figure was itself not negligently high, within the principle expressed in *Bolam* v. *Friern Hospital Management Committee* [1957] 1 W.L.R. 582. In *Mount Banking Corporation Ltd.* v. *Brian Cooper & Co.* [1992] 2 E.G.L.R. 142 the court rejected a submission by the plaintiff that provided they proved negligent errors in a valuer's calculation, they were entitled to recover even though the final valuation was within acceptable limits. The deputy judge rejected the argument that *Corisand Investments Ltd.* v. *Druce & Co.* (1978) 248 E.G. 315 was authority for such a proposition, and held, at p. 127:

> "If the valuation that has been reached cannot be impeached as a total, then, however erroneous the method or its application by which the valuation has been reached, no loss has been sustained because, within the *Bolam* principle, it was a proper valuation."

3.—DAMAGES

(i) Remoteness

(a) *Causation*

Insert new paragraphs after § 3–103:

Imprudent lending

A potentially negligent valuer will usually wish to consider whether the **3–103A** lender can properly be criticised as imprudent. To succeed the negligent valuer will have to prove that some lack of care on the part of the lender (in respect of the lender's business interests) caused or contributed to the loss, despite the negligent valuation. Such a plea, if successful, can result in a finding of contributory negligence, a lack of causation of loss or a concurrent cause of loss. The question of what conduct constitutes imprudent lending is a matter for expert evidence and must be related to the nature of the business carried on by the lender. Different considerations will apply to the lending practices of a building society to those of a secondary bank. For example the Building Societies Act 1986, unlike the Banking Acts, restricts the primary security of a building society to that of freehold or leasehold estate. A building society, unlike a bank, is regulated by the Building Societies Commission, which from time to time issues Prudential Notes that it expects to be observed, and the auditor of a building society has an obligation to report to the Commission in respect of compliance. See Wurtzburg and Mills, *Building Society Law* (looseleaf, Stevens & Sons), Chapters 3, 5 and 14.

In *P.K. Finans International (U.K.) Ltd.* v. *Andrew Downs & Co. Ltd.* **3–103B** [1992] 1 E.G.L.R. 172 the plaintiff was a licensed deposit-taker. The defendant valuer was entitled to proceed on the basis that the plaintiff did not need to be told to verify with its solicitors certain planning assumptions made in the valuation. The deputy judge considered that had he

found the defendant valuer negligent, he would have assessed contributory negligence on the part of the plaintiff in failing to send the valuation
to its solicitors at 80 per cent., but the defendant's argument that such
failure constituted a *novus actus* was rejected.

3–103C   Two general questions have been discussed in recent cases. First, does
the lavishness of the security extinguish the obligation to act as a prudent
lender? In *Kendall Wilson Securities* v. *Barraclough* [1986] 1 N.Z.L.R.
576, Court of Appeal, Wellington, it was held that reasonable prudence
in a solicitor lender advancing trust funds dictated an investigation into
the affairs of the prospective borrower, rather than total reliance on the
security. Contributory negligence in respect of this failure was assessed at
one third. In *H.I.T. Finance* v. *Lewis & Tucker Ltd.* (1993) 9 P.N. 33 the
negligent valuation was £2,200,000. The advance secured on the property
was £1,540,000. Wright J. commented at p. 39:

> "The cushion apparently provided by the property, on the basis of
> the defendant's valuation was accordingly £660,000. In such circum-
> stances, even if the borrowers turned out to be complete men of
> straw, the lenders were entitled to regard themselves as being more
> than adequately covered not merely in respect of the capital sum
> lent, but also any likely loss of interest, and indeed all the costs and
> expenses likely to be incurred in foreclosing upon and realising the
> security . . . it is very difficult to see how such a lender could
> properly be characterised as being imprudent."

However, the judge went on to say:

> "I am not suggesting that the prudent lender, merely because he has
> the comfort of more than adequate security, is entitled to shut his
> eyes to any obviously unsatisfactory characteristics of the proposed
> borrower . . ."

and gave as an example a lender not acting prudently the making of a
loan in circumstances where he had substantial reason for suspecting the
honesty of the borrower. This general approach was followed by Gage J.
in *United Bank of Kuwait* v. *Prudential Property Services Ltd.*, December
10, 1993 (unreported):

> "It seems to me that it is important to bear in mind Mr. Justice
> Wright's observation that the nature and extent of enquiries required
> may vary widely, and that an important factor will be the margin of
> safety provided by the security offered."

3–103D   Secondly, once there is reliance on a negligent valuation is there any
room for contributory negligence by the person who so relies? The

argument that in such circumstances there can be no contributory negligence was expressly rejected in *Kendall Wilson Securities* v. *Barraclough*, *P.K. Finans International (U.K.) Ltd.* v. *Andrew Downs & Co. Ltd.* [1992] 1 E.G.L.R. 172, and by Gage J. in *United Bank of Kuwait* v. *Prudential Property Services Ltd.,* December 10, 1993 (unreported). Phillips J. in *Banque Bruxelles Lambert S.A.* v. *Lewis & Tucker Ltd. and others*, December 21, 1993 (unreported) proceeded on a similar basis. In assessing contributory negligence at 30 per cent., Phillips J. restricted himself to fairly limited grounds, namely that as a prudent lender the bank should have sought and obtained explanations for the substantial differences between the purchase prices of the properties and the reported values. The judgment suggests that had more of the allegations of imprudent lending been material and proved, the percentage deduction would have been much greater. See § 3–146K. In *Nyckeln Finance Company Ltd.* v. *Stumpbrook Continuation Ltd.,* March 11, 1994 (unreported) the plaintiff finance company lent £21m. on a property sold for £23.5m. yet valued by Jackson, Stopps & Staff for £30.5m. The loan, although only 70 per cent. of the valuation, was 90 per cent. of the sale price. Judge Fawcus, sitting as a judge of the High Court, held the plaintiffs to be 20 per cent. to blame for proceeding without satisfying themselves as to the reliability of the valuation. See judgment, p. 29.

(ii) Measure of Damages

In *Reeves* v. *Things & Long*, November 19, 1993 (unreported), Sir **3–110** Thomas Bingham M.R. considered, *obiter* and in a dissenting judgment, appropriate measures of damage where a plaintiff would not have entered into a commercial property transaction had he been properly advised. In particular, the Master of the Rolls considered that a fairer and more accurate assessment of the plaintiff's loss would be achieved by applying the diminution of value test to the date when the defect was discovered, rather than to the date of breach. This would have the effect of taking account of substantial expenditure on improvements. This case is further considered at § 4–176A. A broadly similar argument was rejected by Judge Smout Q.C. in *Hooberman* v. *Salter Rex* [1965] 1 E.G.L.R. 144, discussed at § 3–124.

(a) *Negligent survey or valuation for a purchaser who completes a purchase*

Add to NOTE 90: See also *Reeves* v. *Things & Long*, November 19, **3–124** 1993 (unreported), discussed in § 3–110, above.

Add to NOTE 91: [1991] 1 W.L.R. 1421. **3–125**

Court of Appeal's decision

3–127   Add to NOTE 97: [1991] 1 W.L.R. 1421.

(b) *Relevance of costs of repairs*

3–131   Add NOTE 7a: The decision of the Court of Appeal in *Watts* v. *Morrow*
[1991] 1 W.L.R. 1421 is discussed and criticised by T. Dugdale in "*Watts*
v. *Morrow*: Penalising the House Purchaser" (1992) 8 P.N. 152.

(c) *Negligent survey or valuation for lender who would have lent nothing
with a proper survey or valuation: Swingcastle Ltd.* v. *Alastair Gibson*

Add new paragraphs after § 3–136:

The argument of Sir John Megaw in the Court of Appeal

3–136A   Sir John Megaw held that he was bound by *Baxter* v. *F. W. Gapp &
Co. Ltd.* [1939] 2 All E.R. 752 to dismiss the appeal. He differed from
Neill L.J. and Farquharson L.J., however, in that he would have
dismissed the appeal also on principle. He sought to draw an analogy with
the cases where the plaintiff was a purchaser of a house that had been
negligently overvalued (see § 3–112). In both situations, he said, the
damages have to be calculated by reference to the date when the loss is
incurred. At p. 1236D–E, Sir John Megaw said:

> "The loss is incurred if and when the lender, validly under the loan
> contract, realises the security, and the amount realised is less than
> the amount due under the loan contract, including expenses properly
> incurred, and allowing for all payments made by the borrower. There
> is one important qualification. The valuer should not be liable for a
> greater amount than the amount of his original overestimate of the
> value compared with the true market value as at the date of the
> valuation. Any shortfall in the proceeds of the realisation above that
> amount should not be regarded as being caused by the negligent
> valuation."

3–136B   Sir John Megaw in effect asserts that it is not necessary to draw the
distinction between a no loan or a less loan situation. This implies that a
negligent valuer ought not to have to bear the risk of a fall in the property
market even in a case where but for the negligent valuation, no loan
would have been made. It is respectfully submitted that in cases where no
loan would have been made, Sir John Megaw was in error. His views are
at variance with those of the other two Lords Justices, with the House of
Lords on the subsequent appeal, and with leading textbooks, but have
now begun to receive a degree of first instance judicial support. See § 3–
136D.

Sir John Megaw argues that the time at which the loss is incurred is the **3–136C** time at which the amount realised from the security turns out to be less than the amount due under the loan contract. That cannot be correct, since the loss can be determined immediately after completion of the loan. He then appears to have assumed, although the passage is not entirely clear, that the quantum of the loss is similarly determined by the amount by which the sum recovered from the security falls short of the sum due under the contract. In effect, there is a cap on the quantum of damages payable. On this point, it is submitted, authority is against the argument. The statement that the damages recoverable from the valuer are limited to the difference between the valuer's overestimate and the property's true value, and that any shortfall above that amount should not be regarded as having been caused by the negligence complained of, was put forward without supporting argument. It appears to have been based on an analogy with the situation where the plaintiff has bought a negligently overvalued property. Such an approach is contrary to authority, as was indicated in the judgments of Farquharson L.J., who was sitting with him in *Swingcastle* v. *Gibson*, and O.Connor L.J. in *London and South of England Building Society* v. *Stone* [1983] 1 W.L.R. 1242. It was the approach of Neill L.J. and Farquharson L.J., rather than the approach of Sir John Megaw, that was supported in the House of Lords.

In the House of Lords, Lord Lowry began by citing Lord Blackburn's **3–136D** dictum in *Livingstone* v. *Rawyards Coal Co.* (1980) 5 App. Cas. 25, at p. 39. He then cited:

(a) *Clerk and Lindsell on Torts* (16th ed., 1989), para. 11–45, pp. 670–671; this supports the contention that a mortgagee who can establish that no advance would have been made is entitled to recover the difference between the sum advanced and the sum recovered on sale of the property, plus any consequential losses and expenses;

(b) various passages from *McGregor on Damages* (15th ed., 1988), paras. 1212–1218, pp. 749–753, which argue that:

   (i) claims against valuers by the purchasers of property are to be assessed on a different basis from claims by the mortgagees of property;

   (ii) the relevant sum to be deducted from the amount of the unrecovered loan is not the true value of the property, but the amount that would have been lent if the valuer had not been negligent;

   (iii) the loss of the money advanced may be increased by expenses and reduced by receipts.

At pp. 233F–237, Lord Lowry went on to deal with the interest point, concluding this section of his speech by disapproving *Baxter* as an authority on that issue. At p. 237A he said:

[45]

"The approach of the valuer in this case and the analysis of Neill
L.J., which I have reproduced above, seem to me to be correct."

It is submitted that this statement is of general application to circumstances where a lender proves it would not have lent with the benefit of
non-negligent advice from a valuer. This approach to the assessment of
damages in such a factual situation has been approved and applied:

   (a) by the Court of Appeal in *Baxter* v. *Gapp*;
   (b) by the Court of Appeal in *London and South of England Building
       Society* v. *Stone*;
   (c) by the majority of the Court of Appeal in *Swingcastle* v. *Gibson*;
   (d) unanimously, by the House of Lords in *Swingcastle* v. *Gibson*;
   (e) by the editors of the text books cited;
   (f) by Gage J. in *United Bank of Kuwait* v. *Prudential Property
       Services Ltd.*, December 10, 1993 (unreported);

and, it is submitted, cannot now be overturned without taking a case to
the House of Lords. The views of Sir John Megaw have however received
support from T. Dugdale, "Causation and the Professional's Responsibility" (1991) 7 P.N. 78, and in a later article (1991) S.J. 891 (August 8,
1991). In his judgment in *Banque Bruxelles Lambert S.A.* v. *Lewis &
Tucker Ltd. and others*, December 21, 1993 (unreported), Phillips J.
considered it unfair that negligent valuers should bear the risk of a fall in
the property market. However, he recognised that such a finding was
difficult where no loan would have been made because of the weight of
authority, discussed above. See judgment, p. 141. Judge Fawcus, sitting
as a judge of the High Court cited the views of Professor Dugdale in
Nyckeln Finance Company Ltd. v. *Stumpbrook Continuation Ltd.,* March
11, 1994 (unreported); see judgment, p. 36.

Add new paragraphs after § 3–138:

3–138A   In *H.I.T. Finance Ltd.* v. *Lewis & Tucker Ltd.* (1993) 9 P.N. 33, the
defendant valuers admitted providing the plaintiff lender with a negligently high valuation of certain commercial property. The plaintiff was
created as a lending outlet for and owned by Hillsdown Investment Trust
Ltd. and Kleinwort Benson Ltd., neither of which were parties to the
action. A claim for contractual interest was made on the ground that the
plaintiff was obliged to pay virtually all of the interest it received, or
should have received from its borrowers to its parent companies, and
therefore the loss suffered by the plaintiff was, in accordance with
Swingcastle the sums it owed to its parents. The plaintiff had only one
executive officer, whose salary was paid by a parent company. It had no
other staff, no separate offices, no capital and any residual profits were

passed to its parents. The plaintiff was unable to borrow funds to support its lending activities on the open market but was constrained to borrow from its parent companies.

Wright J. held that the plaintiff had no independence of operation, it **3–138B** was simply a financial arm of its two parents. Examining the underlying realities, the judge concluded that it was the parents who, in truth, provided the money for the loan, through the instrument of the plaintiff and that it was these two companies, rather than the plaintiff, who had suffered the loss that flowed from the negligence of the defendant. As in *Swingcastle* there was no evidence before the judge as to how the parent companies had financed the money that they passed to the plaintiff for onward loan. Nor was there any evidence showing how such money, if not lent to the plaintiff, would have been profitably employed. The judge felt able to take notice of the fact that both parent companies were, or were owned by major public limited companies and that surplus funds would be put to the best available use.

The judge awarded one per cent. over clearing bank base rate simple interest on the fluctuating balance due for the period since the loan was made. See also *G.U.S. Property Management Ltd.* v. *Littlewoods Mail Order Stores Ltd.*, 1982 S.L.T. 533 on the question of arms length transactions. In *Nykredit Mortgage Bank plc* v. *Edward Erdman Group Ltd.*, October 1, 1993 (unreported), His Honour Judge Byrt Q.C. sitting in the Mayor's and City of London Court, awarded the plaintiff interest at its borrowing rate on the money market, it being agreed that such a rate precisely reflected the loss suffered by the plaintiff. The rate varied between 0.25 to 0.4 over LIBOR from time-to–time and was calculated as simple interest on the capital sum lent, £2.45 million, from the date of the advance, giving credit for receipts of capital by way of reduction in the capital sum.

Add new paragraph after § 3–139:

The defendant in *United Bank of Kuwait* v. *Prudential Property* **3–139A** *Services Ltd.*, December 10, 1993 (unreported) argued that the starting point for any assessment of damages was the difference between the highest non-negligent valuation and the defendant valuer's negligent valuation. Gage J. preferred the submission of the plaintiff that the starting point was the correct valuation, as found by the judge. The plaintiff had contracted to obtain from the defendant the correct valuation not the highest non-negligent valuation.

Mortgagor's covenants to repay

Add: The approach of Devlin J. in *Eagle Star Insurance Co. Ltd.* v. **3–141** *Gale and Power* (1955) 166 E.G. 7 was preferred by Phillips J. in *Banque Bruxelles Lambert S.A.* v. *Lewis & Tucker Ltd. and others*, December 21, 1993 (unreported).

(d) *Negligent survey or valuation for lender who would have lent a lesser sum with a proper survey or valuation*

3–143   Replace text of existing paragraph with: A common[45] measure of loss in such cases is:

(*a*) the difference between (i) the advance actually made less any capital recovered, whether by way of repayment by the borrower, or from the sale of the mortgaged property, and (ii) the lesser advance that would have been made, less any capital that would have been recovered in such circumstances; plus

(*b*) any consequential expenses that would not have been incurred in any event; plus

(*c*) interest at an appropriate rate to reflect the loss of use of the additional capital sum advanced, credit being given for any interest payments received by the lender on the additional capital.

Insert after § 3–145:

3–145A   The precise method of assessing damages adopted by Gibson J., although appropriate to the facts in *Corisand*, do not necessarily apply to all situations where a lesser sum would have been advanced by the lender. In particular, Gibson J. did not have to consider any question relating to the value of the property in question, as the lenders had no effective interest in the same.

Insert new paragraphs after § 3–146:

The Banque Bruxelles Lambert decision

3–146A   The question of the measure of damages in a situation where a lesser loan would have been made was considered at length in *Banque Bruxelles Lambert S.A.* v. *Lewis & Tucker Ltd. and others,* December 21, 1993 (unreported). The case, which was of unusual length and complexity, concerned a series of very large loans made by the plaintiff bank where the borrowers defaulted and the bank suffered heavy losses. The bank alleged that certain losses were caused by the negligence of defendant valuers, who had provided negligent over-valuations of the properties. Three valuations were either admitted or were found to have been negligent. A large number of issues were argued and decided, a summary of the more important being as follows:

Liability

3–146B   A valuer who gives an open market valuation without considering the implications of a recent sale is, in the absence of express instructions from the lender, negligent. See judgment pp. 46–52.

Reliance

In order to establish reliance on a valuation, a lender has to do more **3–146C**
than establish that, but for the valuation, they would not have made the
loan. They have to establish that they believed the valuation to be
correct. Therefore, where a natural person does not consider a valuation
correct but would not have made a loan without it (because he needs the
valuation to protect his own position), there will be no reliance. See
judgment, pp. 93–98.

Mortgage indemnity guarantees

Where a lender would not have made a loan without a mortgage **3–146D**
indemnity guarantee, it does not follow that he did not rely on the
valuation. There is no break in the chain of causation. See judgment,
pp. 98–99.

Any recoveries made by a lender from a mortgage indemnity guarantee **3–146E**
fall within the doctrine of *res inter alios acta* and the lender does not
therefore have to give credit. Dealings between the lender and its insurer
are of no relevance in the context of the assessment of the lender's
damages. See judgment, p. 116.

Measure of damages

As discussed above at § 3–141, Phillips J. preferred the view of Devlin **3–146F**
J. in *Eagle Star* to that of O'Connor L.J. in *Stone* that the value of a
borrower's personal covenants to repay have to be taken into account in
assessing damage suffered as a result of a valuer's negligence. See
judgment, p. 102.

A fall in the property market

As discussed above at § 3–136D, Phillips J. decided that his finding that **3–146G**
the bank would have "lent less" permitted him to conclude that the
valuer was not liable for the consequences of the fall of the property
market. This is a difficult conclusion by reason of the weight of authority
against the proposition and the facts of the case. The conclusion can be
justified:

(a) Phillips J. did not consider it fair that a valuer should, in general,
be responsible for the consequences of the fall in the value of the
property market: see judgment, p. 141. Stated thus, the proposition seems reasonable, the valuer does not warrant his valuation to
be good against a fall in the property market, nor does he purport
to foretell such movements. The other side of the argument is why
should the innocent lender, who relies on the negligent valuation
to lend money, bear such risk? If the property market is *rising,* is
that to be computed in favour of the lender?

(b) Phillips J. realised that any such general finding was very difficult on the authorities; see judgment, p. 129. This must be the correct conclusion. See the analysis in § 3–136D, above;

(c) Phillips J. therefore made important findings of fact which arguably justify his finding that the bank was not entitled to recover in respect of such consequences. The more important of these are as follows:

(i) Although the loans would not have been made if there had been competent valuations this would not have been because the bank was not prepared to make lower loans but rather because they would not have been accepted by the borrower/sponsors. (See p. 100 of the judgment.) This finding, that the case was a "lent less" rather than a "no loan," permitted the Judge to distinguish *Stone* and *Swingcastle*. This may be stretching beyond that which is reasonable the simple categorisation of transactions into "lent less" or "no loan." If it was right that the bank would not have made any loans had they received competent valuations, then the transactions were "no loan". However the facts were very complex, and the judge found as he did for reasons that he sets out in detail: see judgment, pp. 100–101.

(ii) The bank relied exclusively on the property market to provide the source of repayment of the loan (see judgment, p. 117) which distinguishes this case from most prudent lending where the primary reliance is placed on the ability of the borrower to repay with reference to the security only for comfort in the event of disaster.

(iii) The loans were 90 per cent. of valuation. Phillips J. found that the 10 per cent. reduction was not to protect against falls in the property market but rather to protect against *competent* errors in the valuation. See judgment, p. 120;

(iv) Neither the bank nor Eagle Star relied on the valuer in respect of the risk of a fall in the property market. See judgment, p. 121;

(v) If this were a case of an "ordinary" loan (by which the Judge meant a loan of 70 per cent.), it would be necessary to take account of the loss of a "cushion" of 30 per cent. of valuation afforded by the fact that the loan was only for 70 per cent.: see judgment, p. 121.

(vi) Damages fall to be assessed not at the dates when the causes of actions arose, but as at the date of judgment. This was because of tort causing damage which was subject to ongoing consequences: see judgment, p. 103.

[50]

The above result meets the broad justice of the case on its facts. **3–146H** However, the penultimate finding of fact has some difficulty of more general application. An attempt to apply all the findings in this case to both "lent less" and "no loan" situations produces difficult results and certain aspects of this judgment may be peculiar to the facts of that case. This part of Phillips J.'s judgment may be contrasted with the approach of Gage J. in *United Bank of Kuwait* v. *Prudential Property Services Ltd.,* December 10, 1993 (unreported):

"The defendant contends that on the non-transaction basis the plaintiff's damages should be limited to the difference between £2.5 million and the highest non-negligent valuation which could be made. The basis for this argument is that the loss should be regarded as occurring at the date of the breach of contract. Any loss over and above this difference is attributable to the fall in the property market and not the breach; alternatively such loss is not foreseeable. The difficulty with this argument . . . is that it runs against the decision in *Baxter* v. *Gapp* [1939] 2 K.B. 291. That decision is clear authority for the proposition that in non-transaction cases the proper measure of damages is the difference between the sum advanced and the sum recovered on the sale of the property, plus any consequential losses and expenses."

Gage J. then considered *London and South of England Building Society* v. *Stone* [1983] 1 W.L.R. 1242 and *Swingcastle Ltd.* v. *Alastair Gibson* [1991] 2 A.C. 223, including in particular the passages set out on p. 282, § 3–137 of the main work. The learned judge concluded:

"In my judgment, it is clear from those passages that the House of Lords was not dealing with the main principle in *Baxter* v. *Gapp* but only a subsidiary issue. The main principle in *Baxter* v. *Gapp* which is a decision of the Court of Appeal, still stands and I am bound by it."

This approach was not followed by His Honour Judge Fawcus, sitting as a judge of the High Court, in *Nyckeln Finance Company Ltd.* v. *Stumpbrook Continuation Ltd.*, March 11, 1994 (unreported) (a "no loan" case) who preferred to follow Phillips J., despite a number of factual distinctions from the *Banque Bruxelles* case. These included a "cushion" of 30 per cent.

Baxter v. Gapp

Phillips J. considered that *Baxter* v. *F. W. Gapp & Co. Ltd.* [1939] 2 **3–146I** All E.R. 752 should no longer be relied on as governing the principles to be applied to the assessment of damages in loan cases. (See judgment, p. 135.) As discussed above at §§ 3–136A and 3–146H, this statement must be regarded as (with respect, at best) *obiter dicta* and has not been followed in other cases. See *United Bank of Kuwait* v. *Prudential Property Services Ltd.*, § 3–146H, and compare with *Nyckeln Finance Company Ltd.* v. *Stumpbrook Continuation Ltd.*, March 11, 1994 (unreported), where *Baxter* v. *Gapp* was distinguished on the ground that it was not considering the factual situation of a collapse in the property market.

Syndication

3–146J   The bank was the lead bank of a syndicate in respect of a number of loans. In certain instances the syndicate was in existence at the time of the loan; in others the bank disposed of a share afterwards. The bank was held not entitled to recover damages on behalf of the syndicate of banks which had lent monies to the borrowers. This was so however the involvement of the syndicate banks came about. (See judgment, pp. 111 and 112.) The judge held that syndication was not *res inter alios acta* (*i.e.* a subsequent event that did not relieve the contract breaker of his obligations in respect of the full amount of the loss initially suffered) and that the bank had not suffered the losses it sought to recover. A consequence was that the syndicate banks should have been parties to the action if they had wished to recover damages. Such a course would have involved formidable difficulties in proving reliance.

Contributory negligence

3–146K   This subject is considered further at § 3–103A. Mortgage indemnity guarantees should be ignored when considering contributory negligence by reason of the principle of *res inter alios acta*. If it is negligent to lend 95 per cent. of a valuation it is so negligent whether or not one is insured. Because of Phillips J.'s finding that the valuer was not liable for the fall in the property market, he did not consider allegations of contributory negligence which went to the issue of whether or not the bank was negligent to take such a risk. (See judgment, pp. 149–150.) The judge noted that lending 90 per cent. of valuation would be imprudent if it were relevant to take into account the risk of a fall in the value of the market. (See judgment, p. 147.) The fact that the borrowers were not putting any of their own funds into the transactions did not mean that the transactions were necessarily commercially imprudent but did mean that they should have been examined with scrupulous care. Phillips J. concluded that the bank, as a prudent lender, should have sought and obtained explanations for the difference between the purchase price of the properties and the reported values. (See judgment, p. 164.) This contributory negligence alone was assessed at 30 per cent.: see judgment, p. 174.

"No loan"/"lent less"

The judge held that the bank would have been prepared to make lower **3–146L** loans, although lower loans would not have been accepted by the borrowers: see judgment, p. 101. This finding distinguished the case from the factual situation in *Swingcastle*. Phillips J. also concluded that the bank relied exclusively on the property market to provide repayment of the loans: see judgment, p. 117. This is an important finding. In virtually all domestic, and some prudent commercial lending, the lender places primary reliance on the ability of the borrower to service the loan. This is especially so in the case of building societies where the terms of the Building Societies Act 1986 imposes a requirement of prudence, (see section 45), and various Prudential Notes issued by the Building Societies Commission make specific reference to the need to ensure that the borrower can service the loan, (see the Commission's Note 1987/1, for example).

Conclusion

These, and other specific findings of fact, were held by Phillips J. to **3–146M** justify the conclusion that the negligent valuer was not liable for the subsequent fall in the property market. The fact that the value of the subject properties subsequently dropped was ignored. In cases that can be brought within the principles expressed by Phillips J., the measure of loss appears to be as follows:

(1) calculate the loss of capital advanced attributable to the valuers negligence; then deduct;
(2) the loss attributable to the fall in the property market, by deducting from:
   (i) the value of the property at the date of valuation;
   (ii) the value of the property at the date of assessment of damages;
(3) plus interest to compensate for the loss of use of that capital sum.

This method was adopted by His Honour Judge Fawcus, sitting as a judge of the High Court, in *Nyckeln Finance Company Ltd.* v. *Stumpbrook Continuation Ltd.*, March 11, 1994 (unreported). On a loan of £21m., the loss attributable to the fall in the property market was calculated to be £17.8m.

This measure will reduce, perhaps substantially, the damages payable **3–146N** by a negligent valuer. A simplified example: £100,000 is lent on a property in fact worth only £50,000. The property is eventually sold for £25,000. The balance is £75,000. From this must be deducted the loss attributable to the fall in the property market: £50,000 − £25,000 =

£25,000. This is deducted from the balance of £75,000 to give a recoverable loss from the negligent valuer of £50,000.

3–146O   It remains to be seen how many cases properly fall within the factual boundaries of this case. What is likely is that most negligent valuers will seek to invoke Phillips J.'s view that it is simply not fair to burden a negligent valuer with responsibility for the consequences of a serious fall in the property market. Whilst doing broad justice to the facts of a very complicated case, a number of the findings of Phillips J. will need to be tested further to determine the boundaries of their application to the more common type of valuer's negligence action. Early indications are that the lead given by Phillips J. is likely to be followed.

3–146P   It is therefore emphasised that there is no judicially approved formula that will apply, without modification, to all factual situations where a lesser loan would have been made. If an absurd result is obtained, then it is very likely that the method of calculation requires adjusting to meet the particular circumstances of the case.

(g) *Other work*

Rent reviews
3–150   Add to text at end of paragraph: The proper calculation of damages resulting from the negligent conduct of a rent review was considered in *Corfield* v. *D.S. Bosher & Co.* [1992] 1 E.G.L.R. 163.

(h) *Inconvenience and discomfort*

Injury to health
3–158   Add: In *Smyth* v. *T.E.W. Huey & J.B. Stelfox* (Northern Ireland) September 16, 1993 (unreported), MacDermott L.J. rejected a claim by the plaintiffs for damages against the admittedly negligent defendant solicitors. The claim was in respect of depression and schizophrenia allegedly caused by the negligent handling of a domestic property purchase. The judge held that the plaintiffs had failed to prove a causal connection between their illnesses and the negligence complained of. In considering the claim for damages in respect of inconvenience, distress and annoyance, the *dicta* of Bingham L.J. in *Watts* v. *Morrow* [1991] 1 W.L.R. 1421 was applied: *ibid*, § 3–152, n. 68.

Quantum of damages
3–160   Add: In *George Buchanan* v. *Newington Property Centre*, 1992 S.C.L.R. 583, the pursuers were obliged to move into rented accommodation for some eight months whilst extensive dry rot was eradicated. The

rented accommodation was in a tall block of council-owned flats where the general level of social amenity was considerably less than that to which the pursuers were accustomed. The second pursuer was frightened to remain in the rented accommodation whilst the first pursuer was at work and so she travelled into central Edinburgh most days. She consulted her doctor. Both pursuers became irritable with one another. Sheriff Scott was satisfied that "the pursuers had a miserable time of it, over a period, as a result of Mr Quinn's breach of duty. Happily, they have recovered. I consider that proper awards of solatium are £800 for the first pursuer and £1,200 for the second pursuer."

In *Heatley* v. *William H. Brown Ltd.* [1992] 1 E.G.L.R. 289 the plaintiffs, a couple with three young children, were compensated for two years of having to live in premises that became wholly unsuitable for family living because of warning of danger. Financial pressures prevented them from moving out. Safe access to the only bathroom facilities available involved leaving the house. This inconvenience was made much worse when the children were unwell and could not be taken outside. Eventually a portaloo was purchased and placed in the inner hall. The health of the second plaintiff was adversely affected and family relationships generally became strained. The judge awarded the first plaintiff £1,500, the second plaintiff £3,000. See also *McLeish* v. *Amoo-Gottfried & Co., The Times,* October 12, 1993, Q.B.D.

(iii) Interest on Damages

Add to NOTE 40: Such interest was awarded in *Heatley* v. *William H.* **3–166** *Brown Ltd.* [1992] 1 E.G.L.R. 289, 297. By contrast, in *McLeish* v. *Amoo-Gottfried & Co, The Times,* October 13, 1993, damages were claimed from the defendant solicitor in respect of the mental distress caused to the plaintiff by reason of his wrongful conviction of a criminal offence. The conviction was quashed by the Court of Appeal. In the solicitors' negligence action Scott Baker J., having regard to R.S.C., Ord. 6, r. 2, and to *Saunders* v. *Edwards* [1987] 1 W.L.R. 1116, exercised his discretion by declining to award any interest on the £6,000 general damages awarded for mental distress.

SOLICITORS

1.—GENERAL

4–01 NOTE 7: Add: see further the Solicitors' Investment Business Rules 1990 and the Financial Services (Conduct of Business) Rules 1990, both of which are reprinted in *The Guide to the Professional Conduct of Solicitors* (6th ed., 1963).

Add to end of text: The latest edition of the *The Law Society Guide* is *The Guide to the Professional Conduct of Solicitors* (6th ed., 1993).

(i) Duties to Client

(a) *Contractual duties*

4–03 Add: If a solicitor considers that the services he is performing for a client are only limited, this should be in writing to avoid misunderstanding,[14a] although it would be sufficient if the client had given written instructions to the solicitor which made the limited nature of the retainer clear.[14b]

NOTE 14a: *Begusic* v. *Clark, Wilson & Co.* (1992) 92 D.L.R. (4th) 273 (B.C.S.C.).

NOTE 14b: *Canada Trustco Mortgage Company* v. *Bartlet & Richardes and Gates* (1991) 3 O.R. (3d) 642 (Ontario H.C.).

4–04 NOTE 19. Add: Clearly, there must be some limited continuing duty, because a solicitor's duty of confidentiality continues, and thus he will have an obligation to decline to accept instructions from a new client because he has acquired knowledge from a former client.

(b) *Duties independent of contract*

NOTE 35. Add: The law in Australia is probably different: see *Wardley* **4–07**
Australia Ltd. v. *Western Australia* (1992) 66 A.L.R. 839, discussed in
Chap. 1, § 1–118.

(c) *Fiduciary duties*
Add: In *Mouat* v. *Clark Boyce* [1992] 2 N.Z.L.R. 559, the New **4–10**
Zealand Court of Appeal accepted the principle of concurrent liability.
The point was not considered by the Privy Council on appeal (reported at
[1993] 4 All E.R. 268).

Replace NOTE 67 by: *Finers* v. *Miro* [1991] 1 All E.R. 182, on which **4–12**
see L. Aitken, "The Solicitor as Constructive Trustee" (1993) 67 A.L.J.
4. For when the Court will act to prevent the risk of a breach of the duty
see *Re A Firm of Solicitors* [1992] Q.B. 959.
Add to end of text: In *Mouat* v. *Clark Boyce* [1993] 3 W.L.R. 1021,
1029A–B, the Privy Council concluded:

"A fiduciary duty concerns disclosure of material facts in a situation
where the fiduciary either has a personal interest in the matter to
which the facts are material, or acts for another party who has such
an interest. It cannot be prayed in aid to enlarge the scope of
contractual duties."

However, an allegation of breach of fiduciary duty may in some
circumstances greatly assist a plaintiff, due to the different principles of
compensation: see *Target Holdings Limited* v. *Redferns, The Times,*
November 24, 1992, discussed at § 4–151, below.

(ii) Duties to Third Parties

(b) *Liability to beneficiaries without reliance*
Add; Macpherson J. came to the same conclusion in *Kecskemeti* v. **4–24**
Rubens Rabin & Co., The Times, December 31, 1992.

The scope of the principle in *Ross* v. *Caunters*
Add: In *White* v. *Jones* [1993] 3 W.L.R. 731, at p. 743B–C, Sir Donald **4–25**
Nicholls V.-C. considered that the principle would apply to a case where
the solicitor is instructed to carry through a transaction of gift to a third
party during the client's lifetime. In *Hemmens* v. *Wilson Browne (A
Firm)* [1994] 2 W.L.R. 323, the settlor instructed the defendant settlor to
draft a document giving the plaintiff the right to call on the settlor to pay
her a sum of money. The document gave the plaintiff no enforceable
rights, as there was no consideration and it was not under seal. Judge

Moseley Q.C. sitting as a judge of the Chancery Division, decided that the solicitors owed no duty of care to the plaintiff, because the settlor was still alive and able to rectify the situation if he wanted to, which he did not. However, the judge considered (at p. 333H) that if a settlor acts on the advice of his solicitor and executes an irrevocable deed of settlement benefiting X instead of the intended Y, the solicitor may owe a duty of care to Y.

Insert a new paragraph after § 4–25:

4–25A   In *White* v. *Jones*,[20a] the Court of Appeal have recently upheld the principle in *Ross* v. *Caunters*. The testator sent a letter to the defendant solicitors with instructions to draft a new will leaving £9,000 to each of the plaintiffs. The solicitors failed to have the will completed in the two months before the testator died. The Court of Appeal approached the question on the basis of the three-stage test in *Caparo* v. *Dickman*[20b] of forseeability, proximity, and whether it was just and reasonable to impose a duty of care. It was just and reasonable to impose the duty for the reason which influenced Megarry V.-C. in *Ross* v. *Caunters*[20c]: if there was no remedy, the testator's purpose would be thwarted but the executor would have no effective remedy, and it was in the public interest that there should be an effective remedy against negligent solicitors. The case is under appeal to the House of Lords.

NOTE 20a. [1993] 3 W.L.R. 731. For comments on the case see J. Blaikie, "The Dilatory Solicitor and the Disappointed Legatee" 1993 S.L.T. 329; H. Evans, "*White* v. *Jones* in the Court of Appeal" (1994) 10 P.N. 169; Fleming, "The Solicitor and the Disappointed Beneficiary" (1993) 109 L.Q.R. 344.

NOTE 20b. [1990] 2 A.C. 605.

NOTE 20c. [1980] 1 Ch. 322H–323A, see the quotation from the judgment of Megarry V.-C. at § 4–19 in the main work.

4–26   NOTE 25. Add: See further S. Baughen, "The Will that Never Was: *Ross* v. *Caunters* Extended" (1992) 8 P.N. 99.

Replace last two text lines by: A similar result was reached in *White* v. *Jones*[27] (for the facts see § 4–24A above). The Court rejected the reasoning of Turner J. at first instance that there could be no duty of care unless the testator's instructions had been formally expressed in a will.

Replace NOTE 27 by: [1993] 3 W.L.R. 731.

(c) *Miscellaneous cases*

Liability without reliance

4–31   Add: In *Welton Sinclair (a firm)* v. *Hyland* (1992) 41 E.G. 112, the plaintiff solicitors had acted for the defendant tenant in the assignment of a lease of a shop to him. The solicitors received a letter from the landlord informing them that he had served on the tenant a notice, under section 25 of the Landlord and Tenant Act 1954, to determine the lease of the shop. The Court of Appeal decided that there had subsequently been a contract between the solicitors and the tenant. They concluded, *obiter*, that in the context of the previous instructions and the landlord's letter, and knowing that there was a strict time-limit on the matter, the solicitors owed the tenants a duty of care either to indicate that they were not going to act or to take immediate steps to ensure that the defendant's interests were safeguarded.

(d) *Duty of care to the other side*

Non-contentious business

Replace NOTE 49 by: (1979) 123 S.J. 860.   **4–33**

Add to NOTE 51: But in *Granville Savings & Mortgage Corp.* v. *Slevin* (1992) 93 D.L.R. (4th) 269, a majority of the Manitoba Court of Appeal held that a solicitor representing a mortgagor owes no duty of care to the plaintiff mortgagee, which had not retained a lawyer.

Insert new paragraph after § 4–33:

Add: The law has been largely settled by *Gran Gelato Ltd.* v. *Richcliff* **4–33A** *Ltd.*[51a] Gran Gelato purchased an underlease from Richcliff. Gran Gelato's solicitors sent enquiries before contract to the second defendants, who were Richcliff's solicitors, which included an enquiry as to whether there were any rights affecting the superior lease which might inhibit the enjoyment of the underlease. The second defendants mistakenly replied "Not to the lessor's knowledge." Richcliff was found liable for this misrepresentation, which Gran Gelato had relied upon to their loss, but not the second defendants. The Vice-Chancellor considered:

> "in normal conveyancing transactions solicitors who are acting for a seller do not in general owe to the would-be buyer a duty of care when answering inquiries before contract or the like."[51b]

The judge did not consider that it was a fair and reasonable reaction that there ought to be a remedy against the solicitor in such circumstances, and he was influenced by the fact that the buyer had a remedy against the seller. However, he was not impressed by the argument that to impose a duty of care on solicitors would expose them to conflicting duties to the client and to the other side.

NOTE 51a. [1992] Ch. 560, Nicholls V.-C. For commentary, see P. Cane, "Negligent Solicitor Escapes Liability" (1992) 108 L.Q.R. 539 and S. Fennell, "Representations and Statements by Solicitors to Third Parties" (1992) 7 P.N. 25.

NOTE 51b. [1992] Ch. 560, 570C–D. See also the dictum of Morritt J. in *CEMP Properties (U.K.) Ltd.* v. *Dentsply Research & Development Corporation* [1989] 2 E.G.L.R. 205, 207.

4–34   NOTE 53. Add: a similar result was reached in *Connell* v. *Odlum* [1993] 2 N.Z.L.R. 257. Under section 21 of the New Zealand Matrimonial Property Act 1978, people who had married or intended to marry could contract out of the provisions of the Act. This required a certificate signed by a solicitor, stating that he had explained the implications of the deed and given her independent legal adive. The defendant solicitor, Mr. Connell, had signed such a certificate for Mrs. Odlum. Six years later, Mrs. Odlum succeeded in setting the deed aside on the basis that it had not been properly explained to her. The New Zealand Court of Appeal concluded that Mr. Connell owed a duty of care to Mr. Odlum in signing such a certificate, and refused to strike out Mr. Odlum's action against the solicitor.

4–36   Delete: from first line of text "directly"; from third line "who were a firm of solicitors".

4–37   Add to NOTE 66: *Al-Kandari* was relied upon in *Jensen* v. *MacGregor* (1992) 93 D.L.R. (4th) 68 (B.C.S.C.), where the court struck out a claim by a husband that the advice of his wife's lawyers to her upon their separation had caused him damage.

Insert after § 4–37:

4–37A   A further and more general exception was established in *Welsh* v. *Chief Constable of Merseyside* [1993] 1 All E.R. 692 (see particularly pp. 702A–703F). The plaintiff was on bail from a magistrate's court for two offences of theft. He was then sentenced in the Crown Court for other matters, and asked for the offences of the theft to be taken into consideration. It was alleged that the Crown Prosecution Service had failed to inform the magistrate's court that the offences had been taken into consideration, with the result that the unsuspecting plaintiff was arrested for failing to answer his bail. The plaintiff sued the Crown Prosecution Service, who applied to strike out his claim on the ground (*inter alia*) that no duty of care was owed to the other side in litigation. Tudor Evans J. refused the application. He considered that the position of a prosecutor in criminal cases is very different from a solicitor in civil litigation; thus, for instance, there was duty to make available to the defence witnesses who can give material evidence but whom the prosecution do not intend to call. Indeed, the judge considered that a duty of care was owed by the prosecutor to the defendant.

(d) *Solicitors liability on undertakings*

Solicitors may be liable for breach of their undertakings. The law is **4–37B**
stated in *Cordery*, pp. 110–112. It should be noted that licensed con-
veyancers have no such liability.

(iii) The Standard of Skill and Care

(a) *The standard of reasonableness*

NOTE 87. Add after the reference to *Elcano* v. *Richmond*: However, **4–43**
the Ontario Court of Appeal ((1992) 3 O.R. (3d) 123) found that the
solicitor had been negligent because he had failed to follow his normal
practice of inserting an interest provision, which was an isolated error.

(b) *General practice as evidence of reasonable skill and care*

Differing practices

Add to NOTE 2: In *Ron Miller Realty Ltd.* v. *Honeywell, Wotherspoon* **4–49**
and Beedell (1992) 4 O.R. (3d) 492 (Ontario High Court), summary
judgment was granted despite the fact that the defendants had filed an
affidavit from an expert suggesting that the mistake made by the
defendants would have been made by most lawyers.

Expert evidence

Add to NOTE 7: A problem that sometimes arises where it is disputed **4–51**
whether the expert evidence is admissible, is that the master or judge in
chambers is not entitled to rule on the admissibility of such evidence:
Sullivan v. *West Yorkshire Passenger Transport Executive* [1985] 2 All
E.R. 134, C.A.

(d) *Mitigating factors*

Add: Solicitors are not justified in providing a second-rate service to **4–54**
clients who were slow in paying their fees (see *F. & G. Reynolds
(Whitchurch) Ltd.* v. *Joseph, The Times*, November 6, 1992).

(e) *Aggravating factors*

Add: If a situation is fraught with danger, particular care may be **4–57**
required. Thus in *Tonitto* v. *Bassal* (1992) 28 N.S.W.L.R. 565
(N.S.W.C.A.) a solicitor was found to be negligent in failing to comply
strictly with the requirements of an option agreement, because it is
common for grantees to seek to avoid a exercise of the option on the
ground that its terms had not been complied with.

Acting for parties with opposed interests

Add to NOTE 31: and also in *Commonwealth Bank of Australia* v. **4–58**
Smith (1992) 102 A.L.R. 453. See further (1992) *Wan* v. *McDonald* 105
A.L.R. 473 (Burchett J.), *Stewart* v. *Layton* (1992) 111 A.L.R. 687
(Foster J.).

Add to text: The Privy Council qualified this general principle in *Clarke Boyce* v. *Mouat* [1993] 3 W.L.R. 1021 at pp. 1027–1029 (following Upjohn L.J. in *Boulting* v. *Association of Cinematograph Television and Allied Technicians* [1963] 2 Q.B. 606 at p. 636). A solicitor may act for two parties whose interests may conflict providing that he had obtained the informed consent of both of them to his acting, which must be given in the knowledge that there is a conflict and that as a result the solicitor may be disabled from disclosing to each party the full knowledge he possesses or from giving some advice.

(iv) Specific Defences to a Claim for Breach of Duty

(a) *Immunity*

4–62   Add to NOTE 51: This applies to an action brought by the other side in litigation, see *Welsh* v. *Chief Constable of Merseyside* [1993] 1 All E.R. 692, 700C (Tudor Evans J.).

(b) *Abuse of process*

Insert new paragraph after § 4–64:

4–64A   In *Walpole* v. *Partridge & Wilson* [1993] 3 W.L.R. 1093, the plaintiff was convicted for obstructing a veterinary officer in the execution of his duty, and he appealed unsuccessfully to the Crown Court. He retained the defendant solicitors to advise him on the merits of a further appeal. He later brought proceedings alleging that the solicitors had failed to lodge an appeal, despite counsel's advice that there were valid grounds for an appeal by way of case stated on a point of law. The Court of Appeal declined to strike out the claim, considering that the initiation of proceedings which challenge the final decision of a court are not necessarily an abuse of process, although they may be. The Court recognised four exceptions to the principle, although the list is not necessarily complete: (1) where the challenged decision was obtained by fraud, collusion or perjury (p. 1100H); (2) where there is sufficient fresh evidence which "entirely changes the character of the case" (p. 1100E–H); (3) where it is alleged that the solicitors failed to prosecute an appeal, as in *Walpole* (p. 1101E–F); (4) in some circumstances, where there has been no decision on the merits such as where the plaintiff has submitted to judgment (p. 1108D). The Court of Appeal therefore doubted *Palmer* v. *Durnford Ford* [1992] 1 Q.B. 483, where the plaintiffs' claim had been struck out. There, the plaintiffs sued their solicitors on the grounds, *inter alia*, that they allowed problems with an expert, who had changed his views shortly before trial, to obscure a partly meritorious claim against the repairer, as a result of which the case was abandoned at trial.[62a]

NOTE 62a. In two recent cases advisers have been found to be negligent in failing to advise their clients in relation to an appeal from a tribunal, although the Court did not address the question of abuse of process: see *Hood* v. *National Farmers Union* [1992] 1 E.G.L.R. 175 (National Farmers Union failing to advise on judicial review in relation to decision of Dairy Produce Quota Tribunal) and *Corfield* v. *D. S. Bosher & Co.* [1992] 1 E.G.L.R. 163 (solicitors failing to advise on appeal from rent review arbitration); see § 4–125A *infra*.

(v) Shared Responsibility

(a) *Contributory negligence*

Add: Contributory negligence is sometimes an issue in actions brought **4–73** by mortgage lenders against solicitors' negligence; guidance can be found in the cases brought against surveyors (see Chap. 3, § 3–103A). It should be noted that in such cases, a claim for breach of fiduciary duty is often made, so that no such defence can be maintained. Similarly, contributory negligence cannot be raised as a defence against a claim in deceit (see *Alliance & Leicester Building Society* v. *Edgestop Ltd.* [1993] 1 W.L.R. 1462, a case brought by a lender principally against a surveyor).

Insert new paragraph after § 4–73:

A recent example of a plaintiff being found contributorily negligent is **4–73A** *Mouat* v. *Clark Boyce*. The plaintiff wished to assist her son by granting a mortgage over her home as security for loans to be made to him, and the defendant solicitors acted for both her and her son. In the initial proceedings a majority of the New Zealand Court of Appeal found the solicitors to be negligent and in breach of fiduciary duty, principally in accepting instructions to act for the plaintiff when there was a serious conflict of interest. In the subsequent hearing [1992] 2 N.Z.L.R. 559 the New Zealand Court of Appeal found the plaintiff 50 per cent. to blame because she failed to act on the defendants' recommendation that she should take independent legal advice, and she told the defendants that she relied upon and trusted her son. On appeal, the Privy Council reversed the finding that the solicitors were liable, and thus it was not necessary to consider the cross-appeal against the finding of contributory negligence (see [1993] 3 W.L.R. 1021 at p. 1029F).

(b) *Apportionment of liability*

Add: Apportionment may arise in other circumstances; for an example **4–74** of the division of fault between a realtor (estate agent) and a conveyancing solicitor, see *Rieger* v. *Croft & Finlay* (1992) 5 W.W.R. 700 (B.C.S.C.).

(v) Solicitor's Liability for Costs

The Rules of the Supreme Court

4–81   Add to NOTE 6: It was relied upon in the criminal case of *R.* v. *Knutsford Crown Court, ex p. Middleweek* [1992] C.O.D. 348 (Div. Ct.).

Add to NOTE 8: and *Sushma Lal* v. *Secretary of State for the Home Department* [1992] Imm. A.R. 303, C.A.

The new changes

Insert new paragraph after § 4–82:

4–82A   There are a number of cases concerning the application of the new section. In *Trill* v. *Sacher, The Times*, November 14, 1992, the defendant's application to strike out the plaintiff's claim had been dismissed, but an order was made for the plaintiff's costs to be paid by their solicitors. The Court of Appeal decided that the solicitors should not pay the costs, because the delay was caused by the slow action of the legal aid authorities and the delay in obtaining counsel's opinion. Similarly, in *Re, A Solicitor (Wasted Costs Order), The Times*, April 16, 1993, no order was made by the Court of Appeal for a solicitor's error of judgment in failing to warn the court or his opponent that he might have to seek at a late stage an adjournment of a hearing because of difficulties with the Legal Aid Board. In *Mainwaring* v. *Goldtech Investments Ltd., The Times*, February 19, 1991, it was accepted by the Court of Appeal that a wasted costs order could be made if solicitors conducted litigation in the knowledge that there was no real likelihood of their ever having their costs and expenses reimbursed by their client, although on the facts of the case no order was made. For further details of the case see the comment by S. Fennell [1991] 7 P.N. 199.

The exercise of the jurisdiction

4–83   Add to NOTE 15: In *Sushma Lal* v. *Secretary of State for the Home Department* [1992] Imm. A.R. 303, the Court of Appeal distinguished *Orchard*. In an immigration case, the solicitor had failed to make full disclosure on an *ex parte* application for leave to move to judicial review. It was held that in the circumstances it was not improper for the Treasury Solicitor to indicate that an application would be made for the solicitor to pay the costs personally if the proceedings were pursued. Similarly, in *Ridehalgh* v. *Horsefield, The Times*, January 28, 1994, the Court of Appeal agreed that threats of applications for wasted costs orders should not be used as a means of intimidation, but if one side did consider that the conduct of the other side was improper, it was not objectionable to inform them.

Add before last sentence: However, the Court of Appeal neither had under the old law nor has under the new law any jurisdiction to order that the costs of solicitors' successful appeals against wasted costs order should be paid out of central funds (see *Steele Ford & Newton* v. *C.P.S., The Times*, May 28, 1993, H.L.).

Insert new paragraph after § 4–83:

Add: In *Wasted Costs Order (No. 1 of 1991), The Times*, May 6, 1992 **4–83A** the Court of Appeal laid down six guidelines for use in criminal cases, which will also be relevant to civil cases. While the decision was made in the context of a wasted costs order against a barrister in relation to his actions in court, the guidelines apply to all legal representatives. See further Chap. 5, § 5–22A below. In *R.* v. *Knutsford Crown Court, ex p. Middleweek, The Times*, March 23, 1992, the Divisional Court stated that judges should seek the assistance of counsel upon their powers, and it was advisable to consider such matters and whether it was necessary to make an order at all.

In *Ridehalgh* v. *Horsefield, The Times*, January 28, 1994, the Court of **4–83B** Appeal gave guidelines on wasted costs orders in civil litigation, which can be summarised as follows:
(1) The Court considered the meaning of "improper," "unreasonable" and "negligent." "Improper" includes conduct which would be a serious and significant breach of a duty of professional conduct. "Unreasonable" describes conduct which is vexatious or designed to harass the other side; the acid test is whether the conduct permits of a reasonable explanation. "Negligence" should be understood in an untechnical way as an error that no reasonably well-informed and competent member of the profession could have made.
(2) A legal representative has not acted improperly, unreasonably or negligently merely because he acted for a party who pursued a claim or defence which was plainly doomed to fail. However, he should not lend his assistance to proceedings which are an abuse of process.
(3) Courts should bear in mind the peculiar vulnerability of legal representatives acting for the recipients of legal aid.
(4) The jurisdiction was not subject to the immunity of an advocate, although a court must make full allowance for the fact that an advocate in court has to make decisions quickly and under pressure.
(5) Where an applicant seeks a wasted costs order against the other side, full allowance has to be made for the respondent lawyers' inability to tell the whole story due to professional privilege.

(6) It was essential to demonstrate a causal link between the improper, unreasonable or negligent conduct and the waste of costs.

(7) In the ordinary way, applications for wasted costs orders are best left until after the end of the trial.

(8) Save in obvious cases, the court should be slow to initiate an enquiry as to whether a wasted costs order should be made, and should leave it to the aggrieved party.

(9) Any procedure should be fair, simple, and summary. The court must be astute to control what could become a new and costly form of satellite litigation.

(10) A legal representative should be given an opportunity to show why an order should not be made, but only when an apparently strong *prima facie* case had been made against him.

(11) The court had a discretion as to whether the legal representative should show cause. This should not be automatic, and the costs of the enquiry compared with the costs claimed will be relevant.

2.—LIABILITY FOR BREACH OF DUTY

4–85 Delete NOTE 27 and replace by: See §§ 4–10—4–12, above.

(i) Giving Wrong Advice

Practical advice

4–90 Add: The more the advice is based on legal considerations, the more likely an error will be found to be negligent. Thus in *Worboys* v. *Cartwright* [1992] E.G.C.S. 110 solicitors advised a client to proceed to sell his farm at auction. The vendor of a farm which the client had purchased was resisting giving a date for vacant possession. Morrit J. held that the solicitors were negligent in their advice, as they had failed to assess the time an action for specific performance would take to be heard and the difficulty of making a decree effective.

(ii) Failing to Give Advice

In respect of matters which he is not asked to investigate or advise upon

4–97 Add to NOTE 61: In *Clark Boyce* v. *Mouat* [1993] 3 W.L.R. 1021, at p. 1028F–G, the Privy Council considered that where the client was in full command of her faculties, and apparently aware of what she was doing, sought assistance of a solicitor in the carrying out of a particular transaction, the solicitor is under no duty to go beyond those instructions by proffering unsought advice on the wisdom of the transaction.

The duty to warn against particular risks

4–101 Add to NOTE 79: *Graybriar Industries Ltd.* v. *Davis & Co.* (1992) 46 B.C.L.R. (2d) 164 (B.C.S.C.).

Explanation of legal documents

Add to NOTE 88: see also *Flandro* v. *Mitha* (1992) 93 D.L.R. (4th) 222 **4–103**
(B.C.S.C.) (conveyancing notary failed to draw unusual rent revision
provision to the attention of the purchaser); similarly, *Rieger* v. *Croft &*
Finlay (1992) 5 W.W.R. 700 (B.C.S.C.).

Advice on matters of business

Add to NOTE 3: see also § 4–97, n. 61. For a useful summary of the **4–108**
law, see *Law* v. *Cunningham & Co. (A Firm)* [1993] E.G.C.S. 126.

Add to NOTE 10: In *Hallmark Financel Insurance Brokers Ltd.* v. **4–109**
Fraser & Beatty (1991) 1 O.R. (3d) 641 (Ontario High Court), a solicitor
interpreted a paragraph in a letter of intent in a particular way when
drafting an agreement to purchase insurance brokers. He sent the draft to
his clients for approval. He was entitled to assume that his clients, who
were experienced businessmen, would take basic steps to ensure that
their instructions were being discharged; furthermore, the clause was a
business component of the transaction rather than a legal one, and so the
solicitor owed no further duty.

Replace NOTE 11 by: (1967) 111 S.J. 399. **4–110**

Add: A different approach was adopted in *Reeves* v. *Thrings & Long*, **4–111**
November 19, 1993, unreported. The plaintiff, who was a businessman,
wished to purchase a hotel. His solicitors, the defendants, advised him
that access to the hotel car park was by licence only with no guarantee of
renewal if and when the licence was brought to an end. A majority of the
Court of Appeal considered that there was no duty to advise the client
upon the commercial implications or risks of the access provisions. Unlike
the clause in *County Personnel Ltd.* v. *Alan R. Pulver & Co.*, the
implications of this clause were obvious.

Insert new paragraph after § 4–125:

(iii) Misconduct of Litigation

After the hearing

If there is a distinct possibility of an appeal, solicitors who represent **4–125A**
clients who have lost litigation should advise them about their rights of
appeal, and about the time-limits for implementing any appeal. Thus in
Corfield v. *D. S. Bosher & Co.* [1992] 1 E.G.L.R. 163, solicitors failed to
advise their clients about an appeal from a rent review arbitration, when
the client had requested a reasoned award which showed that he was
unhappy with the way the proceedings were going. See also *Hood* v.

National Farmers Union [1992] 1 E.G.L.R. 175 (National Farmers Union failing to advise on judicial review in relation to decision of Dairy Produce Quota Tribunal). However, in such cases there might be a defence of abuse of process, see § 4–63.

Settlement

4–130   Add to NOTE 82: Following *Thompson* v. *Howley*, the district court of Western Australia concluded in *Campbell* v. *Gibson* [1992] 8 S.R. (WA) 262:

> "A solicitor who has authority from a client to settle an action may be liable to the client for negligence in the manner of exercising that authority, but not for an error of judgment based on an honest opinion as to the facts or on points of the law of doubtful construction or of new occurrence."

4–131   Add to NOTE 83: See also Chap. 5, § 5–30.

(iv) Misconduct of Non-Contentious Business

(a) *Conveyancing*

4–135   NOTE 97: Delete "909, col. 1" and replace with "911, col. 1."

Add to text at end: Similarly, there may be suspicious circumstances which should prompt further action. Thus in *McManus Developments Ltd.* v. *Barbridge Properties Ltd.* [1992] E.G.C.S. 50 the plaintiff developers purchased property. Between contract and completion a fence at the edge of the property was moved by the adjoining tenants to what they claimed was its true position. The defendants, who were the developers' solicitors, only asked for the fence to be put back. The disputed strip did not belong to the property, and the developers had to buy it back. The Court of Appeal decided that the intrusion should have set alarm bells ringing about whether there was an underlying problem, and the defendant solicitors should have taken further action.

Insert new paragraph after § 4–135:

4–135A   While the standard of care in conveyancing cases is high, it is not absolute, as is illustrated by *Neighbour* v. *Barker* (1992) 40 E.G. 140. The defendant solicitors had advised their clients to have a survey before purchasers, but the advice was not followed. The plaintiffs employed a surveyor after purchase, who informed the defendants that the property their client had just purchased had structural defects. The solicitors advised the plaintiffs to complete the sale, because the consequences of not doing so could be financially disastrous, and that advice was followed.

In fact the vendors had made fraudulent misrepresentations, which would have enabled the plaintiffs to escape from the transaction. However, the Court of Appeal decided that the defendants were not liable, because there was no reason why the defendants should have thought that there was any possible escape from the transaction.

Communicating with the client

Add to NOTE 7: "A person who goes to a lawyer with respect to a land 4–137 transaction is entitled to expect that lawyer to investigate the state of any title that is germane to the matter and to explain to the client exactly what it is that is portrayed by the state of the title" *per* Thackray J. in *Graybriar Industries Ltd.* v. *Davis & Co.* (1992) 46 B.C.L.R. (2d) 164, 181 (B.C.S.C.).

The National Protocol

Add to NOTE 22: For a solicitor's duties with regard to potential 4–141 mortgage frauds, see the Law Society's warning on mortgage fraud, reprinted in the Law Society's *Conveyancing Handbook 1993*, p. 657.

(b) *Investment of money*

Protecting the client

Add to NOTE 22: The Court of Appeal rejected the appeal of the 4–142 solicitors in *Securities and Investment Board.* v. *Pantell* [1992] 3 W.L.R. 897. See further §§ 1–139 and 1–140. See also commentary by S. Fennell in [1992] 8 P.N. 157.

3.—DAMAGES

Add to end of text: If a solicitor fails to disclose material facts in breach 4–151 of fiduciary duty, evidence that the disclosure would not have altered the decision is irrelevant: *London Loan and Savings Co. of Canada* v. *Brickenden* [1934] 3 D.L.R. 465, P.C. Similarly, in *Target Holdings Limited* v. *Referns, The Times*, November 24, 1993, the solicitors, Redferns, had acted for Target who were mortgagees lending £1,525,000 to a borrower. Redferns obtained the mortgage money, and paid it to the borrowers before the transfers of the property were executed rather than at execution. The money was held by Redferns on a bare trust, which was breached by the early payment. A majority of the Court of Appeal concluded that the loss was quantified as the amount paid away in breach of trust, subject only to Target giving credit for any monies recovered by it on the realisation by it of its security. Summary judgment was given for £1,490,000. The loss was caused by the payment of the money in breach of trust, and it was not relevant that the loss may have happened if there had been no such breach; common law principles of causation, fore-seeability and remoteness were not relevant. However, the judgment of Peter Gibson L.J., with whom Hirst L.J. agreed, did state that "It was for Redferns to justify their action or otherwise to show why Target was not entitled to compensation in the sum claimed." It should be noted that in some circumstances the trustee may be able to claim relief under section 61 of the Trustee Act 1925, which was not relied upon by the defendants in *Target*.

(ii) Measure of Damages

Fundamental principle

4–162   Delete last sentence.

Insert new paragraph after § 4–162:

4–162A   Damages are generally, but not invariably, assessed as at the date of breach (see *Zakrzewski* v. *Chas. Oldhams & Sons* (1981) 260 E.G. 1125, Q.B.D.). This principle has been applied in a number of recent cases. In *Amerena* v. *Barling*, May 28, 1993, unreported, the defendant solicitor's negligence caused the plaintiff to enter into an agreement, granting an option over shares, which he would not otherwise have done. The Court of Appeal summarised the law: damages will normally fall to be assessed at the date when the cause of action arose (see *Miliangos* v. *George Frank (Textiles) Ltd.* [1976] A.C. 443, 468 *per* Lord Wilberforce). But this principle will not be applied mechanistically in circumstances where assessment at another date may more accurately reflect the overriding compensatory principle (see *County Personnel Ltd.* v. *Alan R. Pulver & Co.* [1987] 1 W.L.R. 916, 926 *per* Bingham L.J.). The Court was not satisfied that the taking of an assignment of the option two years later at a cost of £1.75m was reasonable. They considered that damages should be assessed at the date of breach, when the benefits receivable under the option agreement were not less than the value of the shares over which the plaintiff had granted an option. Only nominal damages were awarded. Similarly, in *Ricci* v. *Masons* [1993] 38 E.G. 154 (see § 4–173 for the facts), the diminution in the value of the plaintiff's restaurant business caused by the fact that he had obtained a new lease without statutory protection was assessed at the date of breach, rather than at the date the new lease would have been obtained (where the loss to the plaintiff would have been somewhat less) or at the date of trial. In contrast, in *McElroy Milne* v. *Commercial Electronics Ltd.* [1993] 1 N.Z.L.R. 19, the plaintiff was developing industrial property and found a tenant, Imagineering. It instructed the defendant solicitors to draft a lease guaranteed by Imagineering's principal shareholder, Studio. In late 1987, the defendant solicitors negligently failed to make Studio party to the lease. Imagineering, which was in financial difficulties, repudiated the lease. The New Zealand Court of Appeal agreed with the assessment by the trial judge: if the lease had been guaranteed, the plaintiff would have been able to sell the development fully let for NZ$2.25m in January 1989. As a result of the fall in property prices, the plaintiff was instead left with an unsold development at the time of the trial in July 1990 which was worth about NZ$4m. Damages were assessed at NZ$1.25m, relying particularly on *Czarnikow* v. *Koufos* [1969] 1 A.C. 350, H.L. The Court considered that assessing damages at the date of the breach, although the general rule, was artificial and unjust in this case, and that the fall in the property market was foreseeable. See also *Reeves* v. *Thrings & Long*, November 19, 1993, unreported, C.A., discussed at § 4–176A.

Evaluation of a chance

After first four words add NOTE 3a: See further H. Evans, "Damages **4–168** for Solicitors' Negligence: (3) Damages for the Loss of a Chance" (1992) 8 P.N. 85.

(iii) Heads of Damage

(a) *Loss of opportunity to acquire or renew an interest in property*

Add to end of text: In *Ricci* v. *Masons* [1993] 38 E.G. 154, (Mr. L. **4–173** Swift Q.C. sitting as a deputy judge of the Queen's Bench Division), the defendant solicitors failed to serve a notice under section 25 of the Act. Their client, the plaintiff, was able to negotiate for a new lease. The Judge determined that the plaintiff would have obtained a 10-year term with a six-month redevelopment break clause. The plaintiff was awarded the additional cost of the lease which he had to pay, his costs of abortive proceedings and disbursements, and the diminution in the value of his restaurant business caused by the fact that his lease now had no statutory protection.

Replace NOTE 21 by: (1983) 269 E.G. 1040. See § 4–166, above.

Insert new paragraph after § 4–173:

A similar result was reached in unusual circumstances in *Layzell* v. **4–173A** *Smith Morton & Long* [1992] 1 E.G.L.R. 169. The plaintiff's father held an agricultural tenancy. When he died, the defendant solicitors negligently failed to claim a right of succession for the plaintiff pursuant to section 39 of the Agricultural Holdings Act 1986. Schiemann J. found that it was all but impossible to obtain a tenancy on the market equivalent to the one the plaintiff had lost as a result of the defendant's negligence. The plaintiff was awarded the cost of the freehold of an equivalent property, less what he could recover from selling the freehold and taking the leasehold on the terms of the one he had lost. The defendant argued that the plaintiff had only lost a source of cheap housing and a higher income than he would otherwise obtain, both of which could be compensated by applying an appropriate multiplier to the yearly loss. The court rejected this approach, which would have resulted in smaller damages; the plaintiff had expected to be a tenant farmer on his family farm, and the court would award damages to put him in the position he would have been but for the defendant's negligence.

(b) *Diminution in value of property*

Insert new paragraph after § 4–176:

4–176A   In *Reeves* v. *Thrings & Long*, November 19, 1993, unreported, C.A., the plaintiff purchased a hotel where access to the hotel car park was by licence only, and he spent some money rectifying this when the problem came to light four years later. The defendant solicitors were not found to be liable. Sir Thomas Bingham M.R., with whom Simon Brown L.J. agreed, considered three approaches on damages, if it had been established that the plaintiff would not have entered into the transaction. First, damages might be the plaintiff's entire outlay on the purchase and refurbishment of the hotel. This would probably have overcompensated the plaintiff, because whatever he had invested in might have led to loss in the current recession. Secondly, it may have been preferable to apply the diminution in value test at the date when the problem came to light rather than at the date of breach, although there might be additional claims too. Thirdly, the loss may have been calculated as the costs of rectifying the defect when the problem came to light. The Master of the Rolls concluded that it was undesirable to rule on the proper approach to damages in principle, because assessment of damages is ultimately a factual exercise. He stated that this "is an area in which legal rules may have to bow to the particular facts of the case."[29a]

NOTE 29a. Contrast the case of *Amerena* v. *Barling*: § 4–162, n. 94 above.

4–177   After first sentence add NOTE 29b: For a different view see H. Evans, "Damages for Solicitors' Negligence: (2) Diminution in the Value of Property" (1992) 8 P.N. 29.

(c) *Loss of opportunity to bring proceedings*

Cost of the original action

4–187   Add to NOTE 52: 201.

Means of the defendant

Add to NOTE 54: In *Alberta Workers' Compensation Board* v. *Riggins* **4–188**
(1992) 95 D.L.R. (4th) 279, the defendant solicitors settled a personal
injury claim at too low a level. Other Canadian decisions have been
divided about which party had to prove that the judgment was or was not
collectible. The Alberta Court of Appeal considered that the burden lay
on the plaintiff client, but that the defendant solicitor had to place
collectibility in issue first.

(e) *Loss of some other financial advantage*

Inability to recoup money loaned

Delete existing text and replace by: If, through default of the solicitor, **4–195**
the security proves to be deficient, then the normal measure of damages
is "the difference in the value of the security which he had and upon
which he could realise by sale upon the default occurring, and the value
of the security which he was entitled to have, and which he could have
realised by sale upon default occurring."[74] This may be the whole amount
of the loan, as in *Wilson* v. *Tucker*[75] or part only, as in *Whiteman* v.
Hawkins[76] and *Pretty* v. *Fowke.*[77] The principles laid down by the House
of Lords in *Swingcastle Ltd.* v. *Alastair Gibson,*[78] a case concerning
surveyor's negligence, will generally apply to solicitors too.

NOTE 74. *Wilson* v. *Roswell* (1970) 11 D.L.R. (3d) 737 (Supreme Court
of Canada); followed in *Collin Hotels Ltd.* v. *Surtees* [1988] 1 W.W.R.
272 (Saskatchewan C.A.).

NOTE 75. (1822) 3 Stark. 154 (total failure of security). See also
Donaldson v. *Haldane* (1840) 1 Robin 226 (Ct. Sess.); and *Ronaldson* v.
Drummond & Reid (1991) 8 Rettie 767 (Ct. Sess.). The bases for the
awards in these two cases is unclear.

NOTE 76. (1878) 4 C.P.D. 13 (a third party appeared with an equitable
charge for 46 guineas upon part of the security). See also *Campbell* v.
Clason (1838) 1 Dunlop 270 and (1840) 2 Dunlop 1113 (Court of
Sessions).

NOTE 77. (1887) 3 T.L.R. 845: Stephen J. awarded £350 "as the
difference between the value of the security actually obtained, and the
sum which was to be advanced on it" plus £50 as "a round sum in
consideration of arrears of interest and other matters."

NOTE 78. [1991] 2 A.C. 223. See further Chap. 3, §§ 3–134—3–146.

(f) *The cost of putting right the solicitor's mistake*

Add to NOTE 62: *Kyle* is now reported at 1992 S.L.T. 264. **4–199**

(k) *Inconvenience and distress*

Add to end of text: In *McLeish* v. *Amoo-Gottfried & Co., The Times,* **4–215**
October 13, 1993, Scott Baker J. concluded (without the contrary being
argued) that the very essence of a retainer to act for a defendant in a

criminal trial was to ensure his peace of mind. There, the solicitors' negligence caused the client to be convicted and fined £450 for assault and possessing an offensive weapon, before the Court of Appeal quashed the conviction over two years later. The client was awarded £6,000, taking into account the distress he was caused by his loss of reputation.

CHAPTER 5

BARRISTERS

1.—GENERAL

(v) Immunity

(b) *Extent of immunity*

Examples

Add to NOTE 80: *Welsh* v. *Chief Constable of Merseyside* [1993] 1 All **5–20**
E.R. 692, 700C (Tudor Evans J.).

(vi) Abuse of Process

Add to NOTE 82: the principle was applied in the context of civil **5–21**
litigation in *Palmer* v. *Durnford Ford* [1992] 1 Q.B. 483 which has
subsequently been doubted in *Walpole* v. *Partridge & Wilson* [1993] 3
W.L.R. 1093, C.A. See further Chap. 4, § 4–64A.

Add to NOTE 91: See also *Walpole* v. *Partridge & Wilson* [1993] 3
W.L.R. 1093, C.A.

(vii) Liability for Costs

Insert new paragraphs after § 5–22:

In *Wasted Costs Order (No. 1 of 1991), The Times*, May 6, 1992 the **5–22A**
Court of Appeal laid down guidelines for use in criminal cases. They
require some qualification for use in civil cases. The Costs in Criminal
Cases (General) (Amendment) Regulations (S.I. 1991 No. 789) deter-
mined much of the second and third guidelines, (see also *Practice
Direction (Crime: Costs)* [1991] 1 W.L.R. 498) and the third guideline

cannot be applied without amendment to civil litigation. Furthermore, this case concerned a judge initiating the wasted costs procedure, and the guidelines need some modification for a situation where the opposing party makes an application for wasted costs. Finally, the court made clear that the guidelines are not comprehensive. Subject to these qualifications, the guidelines will be relevant to civil cases, and are included in the first supplement to *The Supreme Court Practice* 1993. They can be summarised as follows:

1. The wasted costs jurisdiction is draconian, and thus the court must formulate the complaint carefully and concisely.
2. Where necessary, a transcript of the part of the proceedings under discussion should be available. A transcript of any wasted costs hearing should be made (this is required by the 1991 Regulations).
3. A defendant should be present if it was in his interests, especially if the matter might affect the course of his trial. Other parties may make representations, and it might be appropriate for counsel for the Crown to be present.
4. The court recommended a three-stage test:

   "(i) Had there been an improper, unreasonable or negligent act or omission? (ii) As a result had any costs been incurred by a party? (iii) If the answers to (i) and (ii) were yes; should the court exercise its discretion to disallow or order the representative to meet the whole or any part of the relevant costs, and if so what specific sum was involved?"

5. It was inappropriate to propose any deal. The judge should state his complaint, invite comments, and make a ruling.
6. The judge had to specify the sum to be ordered or if that was impossible substitute an alternative procedure.

5–22B   In *Ridehalgh* v. *Horsefield, The Times*, January 28, 1994, the Court of Appeal gave guidelines on wasted costs orders in civil litigation; see Chap. 4, § 4–83B. Six appeals concerning wasted costs orders were consolidated. One of the appeals, *Antonelli* v. *Wade Gery Farr,* concerned a barrister whose conduct of a trial was impaired because she had accepted the brief at a very late stage. The Court of Appeal held that in accepting the brief, counsel was acting properly in accordance with the "cab rank" rule. The court rejected each of the specific criticisms of counsel and set aside the wasted costs order made by the judge.

2.—LIABILITY FOR BREACH OF DUTY

5–30   See also Chap. 4, § 4–131.

CHAPTER 6

MEDICAL PRACTITIONERS

1.—GENERAL

(ii) Duties to Third Parties

Add to end of text: For the opposite view in relation to *Tarasoff*, see **6–11** M. Jones, *Medical Negligence* (1991), pp. 42–44.

Unborn children

Add to end of text: Section 1A of the Congenital Disabilities (Civil **6–12** Liability) Act 1976 was added by section 44 of the Human Fertilisation and Embryology Act 1990. This in effect extends the provisions of section 1 to children born as a result of artificial insemination. Subject to restrictions set out, such children can sue for disabilities caused by negligence prior to the artificial insemination.

The decision of Potts J. in *B.* v. *Islington Health Authority* and the decision of Phillips J. in *De Martell* v. *Merton & Sutton Health Authority* have now been upheld by the Court of Appeal: [1993] Q.B. 204. In *X. and Y.* v. *Pal* (1992) 3 Med.L.R. 195 (discussed at (1993) 1 Med.L.Rev. 119) the New South Wales Court of Appeal held that an obstetrician and gynaecologist treating a woman owed a duty of care in tort to her future child, who had not been conceived at the time of the treatment. See further A. Whitfield, "Common Law Duties to Unborn Children" (1993)

[77]

1 Med.L.Rev. 29. The development of criminal liability for reckless ante-natal neglect which leads to post-natal death is mooted by P. R. Glazebrook at [1993] C.L.J. 20.

(iii) The Standard of Skill and Care

Insert new paragraph after § 6–15:

6–15A   In *Airedale N.H.S. Trust* v. *Bland* [1993] 2 W.L.R. 316 the House of Lords held that the *Bolam* test applies to the withdrawal of medical treatment from a patient who is unable to consent thereto, even where withdrawal will lead to the death of the patient. The defendant Bland was in a persistant vegetative state from which he would not recover. The hospital and physicians responsible for attending on him sought and were granted declarations that they might lawfully discontinue medical treat-ment and care designed to keep him alive, including artificial ventilation, nutrition and hydration. It was decided (1) that a medical practitioner is under no duty to provide medical treatment and care to a patient who is unable to benefit therefrom, (2) that the *Bolam* test applies to determine whether treatment and care is beneficial to, or in the best interests of, a patient who is unable to consent to their discontinuance (see *per* Lord Keith at p. 362E, Lord Goff at p. 373D–E, and Lord Browne-Wilkinson at p. 385F–G). Since there was a responsible medical opinion that neither life in a persistent vegetative state with no prospect of recovery nor the measures necessary to sustain life in that state were of benefit to Bland, those measures could lawfully be withdrawn. Like reasoning has been applied in comparable cases in New Zealand (*Auckland Area Health Authority* v. *Att.-Gen.* [1993] 1 N.Z.L.R. 235 (High Court of New Zealand)) and in South Africa (*Clarke* v. *Hurst* (1992) 4 S.A. 630). The House of Lords in *Bland* stated that it is desirable that the approval of the court in similar cases be sought as a matter of routine. This requirement is inconsistent with the corollary of the reasoning set out above (expressly recognised by the House of Lords), namely, that a doctor is under a positive duty to discontinue treatment of a patient incapable of consent where the continuance of treatment is no longer in the best interests of the patient, and Lord Goff hoped that it might soon be relaxed. The application of the *Bolam* principle in this context is strongly criticised by J. Finnis in "Bland: Crossing the Rubicon?" (1993) 109 L.Q.R. 329, and see further criticism by J. Keown in "Doctors and Patients: Hard Case, Bad Law, 'New Ethics' " [1993] C.L.J. 209. It is noteworthy that while the application of the *Bolam* principle is thus extended in England and Wales, its ambit has been significantly restricted in Australia: see *Rogers* v. *Whitaker* (1992) 109 A.L.R. 625; (1993) 4 Med.L.R. 79 (High Court of Australia), discussed at § 6–116B below.

(iv) General and Approved Practice

(a) *Acting in accordance with general and approved practice*

Add to end of text: A more recent illustration of the principle is **6–30** afforded by *Burgess* v. *Newcastle Health Authority* (1992) 3 Med.L.R. 224. The plaintiff suffered injuries following a bilateral shunt operation. However, the technique which the registrar had adopted was acceptable to a widely respected body of neurosurgeons, and thus the claim for negligence was dismissed.

Insert new paragraph after § 6–35:

There have been further and more recent indications that the courts are **6–35A** willing, in exceptional cases, to find a medical practitioner negligent notwithstanding his compliance with the general and approved practice. In *Hucks* v. *Cole* (1968) 112 S.J. 483, Sachs L.J. said:

> "When the evidence shows that a lacuna in professional practice exists by which risks of grave danger are knowingly taken then however small the risk the court must anxiously examine the lacuna, particularly if the risk can be easily and inexpensively avoided. If the court finds on the analysis of the reasons given for not taking those precautions that in the light of current professional knowledge there is no proper basis for the lacuna and it is definitely not reasonable that those risks should have been taken its function is to state that fact and when necessary to state that it constitutes negligence."

This approach was approved, *obiter*, by the majority of the Court of Appeal in *Bolitho* v. *City and Hackney Health Authority* (unreported, December 15, 1992). Dillon L.J. said that the court would apply the approach of Sachs L.J. in *Hucks* v. *Cole* and,

> ". . . reject medical opinion on the ground that the reasons of one of the groups of doctors does not really stand up to analysis if the court, fully conscious of its own lack of medical and clinical experience, was nonetheless clearly satisfied that the views of that group of doctors were *Wednesbury* unreasonable, *i.e.* views which no reasonable body of doctors could have held."

This deployment of the *Bolam* test as a rule of evidence, relevant to the question whether a particular established practice exposes the patient to an unacceptable risk, rather than a rule of law as to the standard of care in medical negligence cases was considered and applied in *Defreitas* v. *O'Brien* (1993) 4 Med.L.R. 281, where His Honour Judge Byrt used the standards of one body of opinion to test the reasonableness of another, equally distinguished, but conflicting school of thought. See also *Rogers*

v. *Whitaker* (1992) 109 A.L.R. 625, (1993) 4 Med.L.R. 79 (High Court of Australia), discussed at § 6–116B, below.

(vi) *Res Ipsa Loquitur*

Application of the maxim to professional negligence

6–48 Add to NOTE 88: But see *Lindsay* v. *Mid-Western Health Board* [1993] I.L.R.M. 550, where the Irish Supreme Court held that the plaintiff's failure to return to consciousness after a routine operation required explanation. The plaintiff was unable to point to any precise instance of negligence but was entitled to rely upon the maxim *res ipsa loquitur*. The defendant escaped liability by showing that all reasonable care had been taken, and was not required to prove the probable cause of the plaintiff's condition. *Cf. Thompson Estates* v. *Byrne* (1993) 114 N.S.R. (2d) 395 (Court of Appeal of Nova Scotia), where a patient under intensive care removed tubes from her body and suffered brain damage before she was retubated. She was not entitled to rely upon the maxim: since she was able to disturb her tubation, it was not under the sole management of the defendant hospital and her pre-existing condition was part of the cause of her injury, which could therefore have happened without negligence.

6–50 Add to end of text: for an example of the application of the maxim to a case of negligent failure by a health authority to operate a safe system of care, see *Bull* v. *Devon Health Authority* (1993) 4 Med.L.R. 117.

(vii) Consent to Treatment

6–52 Add to end of text: However, where a child who is "*Gillick* competent" declines to consent to treatment, his parents can do so on his behalf. The court can also consent on his behalf: see *Re W. (A Minor) (Medical Treatment: The Court's Jurisdiction)* [1993] Fam. 64, discussed by J. Eekelaar at (1993) 109 L.Q.R. 182 and by M. Mulholland at (1993) 9 P.N. 21. However, the Court will not order that a particular medical procedure be administered where consent to treatment is forthcoming from the patient or from those with power to consent upon his behalf. The decision as to the appropriate treatment in the best interests of the patient is for his attending doctors, and not for the court: see *Re J. (A Minor) (Child in Care: Medical Treatment)* [1993] Fam. 15.

Insert new paragraphs after § 6–54:

The Jehovah's Witness cases

6–54A It follows from the above discussion that a patient of full age and capacity can effectively refuse medical treatment, even when it is necessary to save his life. Jehovah's Witnesses may do this when the medical treatment involves blood transfusion. See, *e.g. Malette* v. *Shulman* (1991) 2 Med.L.R. 162, discussed in § 6–54, above. However, special circumstances may exist which justify the continuance of medical treatment, despite refusal. For example, the refusal of treatment might have been expressed whilst the plaintiff was under a misapprehension as to the consequences. In *Re T. (Adult: Refusal of Treatment)* [1993] Fam. 95, T, a pregnant woman, who had had links with Jehovah's Witnesses, was injured in a road traffic accident and taken to hospital. T said that she did not want a blood transfusion. However, she said this at a time when she was under the influence of her mother (a Jehovah's Witness) and when a doctor had advised her that there were other procedures available. On the following day a caesarian section was performed. The baby was stillborn, T's condition deteriorated and a blood transfusion became essential. The Court of Appeal upheld a declaration that it was not unlawful to administer a blood transfusion to T. The Court specifically approved the decision of the Ontario Court of Appeal in *Malette* v. *Shulman*. But it held that in the present case T's refusal was not effective, because at the time (*a*) she was under the influence of her mother and (*b*) she believed that alternative treatments would suffice. In *Airedale N.H.S. Trust* v. *Bland* [1993] 2 W.L.R. 316 (discussed at § 6–15A, above) the House of Lords noted that the patient had expressed no wish as to his treatment should he become dependent upon artificial life-support systems before he became unable to do so, but would clearly have weighed such advance directions, had they been given, in considering whether continuance of treatment was in his best interests. For further discussion of anticipatory directions as to medical care, see C. Brennan, "The Right to Die" (1993) 143 New L.J. 1041.

Another special circumstance which would justify overriding the refusal **6–54B** of treatment would be the need to save the life of the patient unable to consent, or of another. Thus in *Re S. (Adult: Refusal of Treatment)* [1993] Fam. 123, the President of the Family Division granted a declaration that a caesarian section could be performed on a woman, despite her refusal on religious grounds, in order to save the life of the baby. The implications of the decision are discussed by K. Stern in "Court-Ordered Caesarian Sections: In Whose Interests?" (1993) 56 M.L.R. 238. In *Re O. (A Minor)* (1993) 4 Med.L.R. 272, the parents of O, an infant suffering respiratory distress syndrome, refused to consent to the transfusion of blood to O on religious grounds. Johnson J. overrode their refusal, authorising a transfusion in the event that O's condition deteriorated to the point where, in the opinion of his doctors, a transfusion was necessary to avoid damage to his vital organs. Similarly, in *Secretary, Department of Immigration, Local Government and Ethnic Affairs* v. *Gek Bouy Mok* (unreported, 1993), the Supreme Court of New South Wales relied upon the decision in *Re F.* and authorised the force-feeding of detainees on hunger-strike (see commentary at (1993) 67 Aus.L.J. 630).

6–55   Add to NOTE 23: For a recent decision on the effect of a general consent form where a type of anaesthesia was used the risks of which had not been explained to the patient, see *Davies* v. *Barking, Havering and Brentwood H.A.* (1993) 4 Med.L.R. 85.

Sterilisation without consent

6–56   Add to end of text: For a comparative discussion of the law on sterilisation of mentally handicapped women in England and Australia, see N. Cica, "Sterilising the Intellectually Disabled: The Approach of the High Court of Australia in *Department of Health* v. *J.W.B. and S.M.B.*" (1993) 1 Med.L.Rev. 186. Cica criticises the use of the *Bolam* principle in the "best interests" test formulated by the House of Lords in *Re F.* as paying excessive regard to the opinion of medical practitioners on the social issues which bear upon the lawfulness of a proposed sterilisation.

Insert new paragraph after § 6–56:

6–56A   In *Re F.* the House of Lords referred to a "special category" of medical procedures the performance of which on those incapable of consent would, as a matter of good practice, require court approval. However, very little guidance was given as to the criteria for deciding which procedures fall into this category. In both *Re B.* and *Re F.* the court rejected as unhelpful any distinction between therapeutic and non-therapeutic medical treatment in deciding whether a proposed sterilisation is lawful. The distinction has assumed procedural significance, however, as a starting point for determining when the court's approval should be sought for medical treatment of those unable to consent. Thus a declaration that the performance of a hysterectomy on a mentally disabled woman for medical (therapeutic) reasons was lawful, even though its effects would include sterility, was refused as unnecessary in *Re G.F. (Medical Treatment)* (1993) 4 Med.L.R. 77, and in *Re R. (A Minor) (Medical Treatment)* [1992] 2 F.L.R. 585. Similarly, a declaration will be refused in clear cases: see *Re H. (Mental Patient)* (1993) 4 Med.L.R. 91 (the performance of invasive diagnostic procedures upon an adult schizophrenic); *Re S.G. (A Patient)* (1993) 4 Med.L.R. 75 (performance of an abortion upon a mentally handicapped woman did not require authorisation by the court, since adequate safeguards were contained in the provisions of the Abortion Act 1967). By contrast, approval will almost always be required for non-therapeutic sterilisation of the mentally handicapped: see *Re W. (A Patient)* [1993] 1 F.L.R. 381 and *Practice Note (Sterilisation: Child)* [1993] 3 All E.R. 222.

Add to NOTE 40: In *Davis* v. *Barking, Havering and Brentwood H.A.* **6–58** (1993) 4 Med.L.R. 85, the argument that separate consent would be required for each type of anaesthesia used was rejected, partly because an approach which required consent for each aspect of treatment (a "sectional" approach) would encourage the bringing of actions in trespass rather than in negligence.

(viii) Allied Professions

Add to end of text: The Medicinal Products: Prescription by Nurses, **6–60** etc. Act 1992 will enable nurses, midwives and health visitors to prescribe such drugs as may be specified in regulations. The organisation of those three professions is now being restructured pursuant to the Nurses, Midwives and Health Visitors Act 1992 (discussed by N. Fletcher at (1992) 8 P.N. 94).

(ix) Hospitals

Primary liability
Add to end of text: In *Bull* v. *Devon Health Authority* (1993) 4 **6–63** Med.L.R. 117, the defendant health authority's failure to operate an efficient and reliable system for securing the attendance of experienced doctors to deal with crises arising in the course of delivery of children was held to be negligent.

Structure of the National Health Service
Add to end of text: For an analysis of the health care markets **6–67** introduced into the National Health Service in 1991 and of the response of the medical profession, see F. Miller, "Competition Law and Anticompetitive Professional Behaviour Affecting Health Care" (1992) 55 M.L.R. 453. The possibility that the new structure of the health service will allow the formulation of new species of negligence claims is discussed by C. Newdick in "Rights to NHS Resources" (1993) 1 Med.L.R. 53.

(xi) Medical Disaster Litigation

Pertussis
Add to end of text: The Canadian courts have come to a similar **6–71** conclusion to that of Stuart-Smith L.J. on the "general causation" issue: see *Rothwell* v. *Raes* (1990) 76 D.L.R. (4th) 280. In *Best* v. *Wellcome Foundation Ltd.* [1992] I.R.L.M. 609, it was an excessively potent (and so excessively toxic) batch of the vaccine which was found to have been negligently released by the defendant manufacturer and to have caused permanent brain damage when administered to the plaintiff.

[83]

Opren

6–74   Add to end of text: The decision of Hidden J. on the "Opren" limitation issues has been largely upheld by the Court of Appeal: *Nash* v. *Eli Lilly & Co.* [1993] 1 W.L.R. 782. The Court noted that there may well be a "strong case" for legislative action to provide a jurisdictional structure for such group actions. However, the courts could not devise special rules for group medical actions in relation to the exercise of discretion under section 33 of the Limitation Act 1980.

Comment

6–78   Add to end of text: In the benzodiazepine litigation the Court of Appeal stressed the importance of cut-off dates in group litigation. A substantial number of claimants in respect of the drug Halcion sought to participate in the group action after the cut-off date which had been set. Despite special circumstances affecting those claimants, Kennedy J. refused to extend the cut-off date and the Court of Appeal upheld such refusal: *A.B.* v. *John Wyeth & Brother Ltd.* (1993) 4 Med.L.R. 1. The irrecoverable costs of defending a multi-plaintiff action, especially when the majority of those plaintiffs have Legal Aid, may be overwhelmingly disproportionate to the benefit likely to be derived by each plaintiff. In *A.B.* v. *John Wyeth & Brother Ltd. (No. 2)*, *The Times*, December 1, 1993 while disapproving in general the application of a cost-benefit analysis at an interlocutory stage in group litigation, the Court of Appeal nevertheless upheld the decision of Kennedy J. to strike out claims against prescribers of benzodiazepine. Such claims were made in the alternative to those against manufacturers of the drugs, to be pursued if the claims against the manufacturers failed. The damages recoverable by the plaintiffs would then be modest but the expense to the defendants great. The degree of injustice to the defendants indicated that the claims should be struck out as vexatious and an abuse of process.

2.—LIABILITY FOR BREACH OF DUTY

(i) Failing to Prevent Illness

6–86   Add to NOTE 8: In *Ter Keuzen* v. *Korn* (1993) 81 B.C.L.R. (2d) 39, the defendant's failure to take adequate precautions against the transmission of sexually transmitted diseases by artificial insemination procedures meant that he was liable when the plaintiff thereby contracted the HIV virus, even although the defendant was unaware of the risk of infection with HIV by this route. By contrast, the likely difficulty of establishing liability for transmission of the HIV virus from medical staff to a patient is discussed by M. Mulholland in "AIDS, HIV and the Health Care Worker" (1993) 9 P.N. 79.

(ii) Failing to Attend or Examine a Patient

Add to NOTE 14: For a decision to similar effect concerning a general **6–87** practitioner, see: *Stockdale* v. *Nicholls* (1993) 4 Med.L.R. 191.

Add to NOTE 15: See also *Durrant* v. *Burke* (1993) 4 Med.L.R. 25 (a **6–88** general practitioner who had given adequate and proper instructions for the care of a sick infant to its mother was not under a duty to visit to ensure that his instructions were followed); *Stacey* v. *Chiddy* (1993) 4 Med.L.R. 216, for the facts of which see § 6–94, below.

(iii) Wrong Diagnosis

Add to end of text: In *Phillips* v. *Grampian Health Board* (1991) 3 **6–92** Med.L.R. 16 the defendants' failure to diagnose a relatively uncommon case of testicular cancer was held not to amount to negligence.

Add to end of text: In *Stacey* v. *Chiddy* (1993) 4 Med.L.R. 216, the **6–94** Supreme Court of New South Wales found negligent a general practitioner who failed to examine a palpable breast abnormality in the plaintiff, in circumstances where such examination would have confirmed or refuted his provisional diagnosis, although possibly via referral to a specialist.

(iv) Error in the Course of Treatment

The first question
Add to end of text: The choice of one procedure in preference to **6–96** another which in the event would have proved more beneficial (or less injurious) to the plaintiff is not negligent provided that all relevant factors and available evidence bearing on the decision have been properly considered: see, for example: *Hinfey* v. *Salford Health Authority* (1993) 4 Med.L.R. 143; *Darley* v. *Shale* (1993) 4 Med.L.R. 161 (Supreme Court of New South Wales).

Add to NOTE 74: See also *Cherekwayo* v. *Grafton* (1993) 84 Man.R. **6–103** (2d) 81 (failure to provide suitable post-operative care after breast implantation surgery led to the need for emergency corrective surgery); *Brewer* v. *Wade* (1993) 131 N.B.R. (2d) 109 (failure by dentist to treat and ensure follow-up examinations of plaintiff's unusual tooth disease).

Insert new paragraph after § 6–103:

With the growing panoply of available medical treatments, cases **6–103A** sometimes arise where medical practitioners attempt to treat the incurable or embark on treatment which is worse than the original disability.

Thus before considering whether the method of treatment was negligent, it must sometimes be asked whether medical intervention can be justified at all. The fact that the patient or his parent has consented is not a defence, in circumstances where no reasonably competent medical practitioner would have proceeded at all. In *Doughty* v. *North Staffordshire Health Authority* (1992) 3 Med.L.R. 81 the plaintiff was born with a birthmark on her face. A plastic surgeon employed by the defendants carried out 11 to 13 operations during her childhood. As a result there was a considerable area of scarring on her face and the birthmark remained visible. The defendants were held liable on the basis that no body of reasonably competent medical opinion would have exposed the plaintiff to that course of plastic surgery.

(vi) Failing to Explain Treatment or Warn

Canadian law

6–109   Add to end of text: *Ciarlariello* v. *Schachter* is now also reported at (1991) 76 D.L.R. (4th) 449. The concept of informed consent in *Reibl* v. *Hughes* has been adopted as the correct approach in Ireland: see *Walsh* v. *Family Planning Services Ltd. and Kelly* (1993) 11 I.L.J. 90 (Supreme Court of Ireland).

English law

6–115   Add to NOTE 23: For further academic criticism of *Sidaway*, see Giesen and Hayes, "The Patient's Right to Know—A Comparative View" (1992) An.-Am.L.R. 101.

Insert new paragraph after § 6–116:

Australian law

6–116A   The approach of the English courts to the standard of care in disclosure cases did not commend itself to the courts of Australia. The Supreme Court of South Australia in *F.* v. *R.* (1983) 33 S.A.S.R. 189 and in *Battersby* v. *Tottman* (1984) 35 S.A.S.R. 557 (upheld on appeal (1985) 37 S.A.S.R. 524), the New South Wales Supreme Court in *H.* v. *Royal Alexandra Hospital for Children* [1990] Aust. Tort Reports 81–000 and the New South Wales Court of Appeal in *Albrighton* v. *Royal Prince Alfred Hospital* [1980] 2 N.S.W.L.R. 542 rejected the notion that the *Bolam* test determined as a matter of law the appropriate standard of care in cases concerning the provision of advice and information to patients. In *F.* v. *R.* King C.J. said:

"But professions may adopt unreasonable practices, particularly as to disclosure, not because they serve the interests of the clients, but because they protect the interests or convenience of members of the profession. The court has an obligation to scrutinise professional practices to ensure that they accord with the standard of reasonableness imposed by law."

In each of the cases cited above the plaintiff failed on liability, so that the discussion on *Bolam* may be regarded as *obiter*.

In *Rogers* v. *Whitaker* (1992) 109 A.L.R. 625, (1993) 4 Med.L.R. 79, **6–116B** the plaintiff was almost blind in her right eye owing to an injury suffered in childhood. The defendant, an ophthalmic surgeon, offered an operation to remove scar tissue from the right eye. He said that the operation would improve the appearance of the right eye and also, probably, restore some of its vision. Despite the plaintiff's incessant questioning about possible complications of the operation, the defendant failed to warn the plaintiff of the very small risk (1 in 14,000—or slightly greater where, as here, there had been an earlier penetrating injury to the eye operated upon) although he was aware of that risk. If warned of the risk, the plaintiff would not have consented to the operation. The defendant carried out the operation with reasonable skill and care. Unfortunately, the operation did not achieve the intended improvement to the right eye, but did lead to sympathetic ophthalmia in the left eye, leaving the plaintiff almost totally blind.

The trial judge, the New South Wales Court of Appeal and the High **6–116C** Court of Australia all held that the defendant was liable for failing to warn the plaintiff of the risk of sympathetic ophthalmia. It was accepted that the failure to give such warning accorded with a practice accepted as proper by many reputable practitioners, but it was held that the *Bolam* test was inapplicable. In the single judgment given by five of the six judges in the High Court, the reasoning was as follows:

(i) There is a fundamental difference between (a) diagnosis and treatment and (b) provision of information and advice.

(ii) In the case of diagnosis and treatment "responsible professional opinion will have an influential, often a decisive role to play."

(iii) The question whether the patient was given all relevant information does not generally depend upon medical standards or practices.

(iv) A doctor has a duty (subject to the therapeutic privilege) to warn his patient of a material risk inherent in proposed treatment.

(v) "A risk is material if, in the circumstances of the particular case, a reasonable person in the patient's position, if warned of the risk, would be likely to attach significance to it or if the medical practitioner is or should be reasonably aware that the particular patient, if warned of the risk, would be likely to attach significance to it."

(vi) In this case, the plaintiff had incessantly questioned the defendant as to, amongst other things, possible complications.

(vii) The risk of sympathetic ophthalmia was material because "a reasonable person in the patient's position would be likely to attach significance to the risk, and thus required a warning."

The decision in *Rogers* is discussed by D. Chalmers and R. Schwartz, in "*Rogers* v. *Whitaker* and Informed Consent in Australia: A Fair Dinkum Duty of Disclosure" (1993) 1 Med.L.R. 129; see also F. A. Trinidade, "Disclosure of Risks in Proposed Medical Treatment" (1993) 109 L.Q.R. 352. D. Cassidy, in "Malpractice—Medical Negligence in Australia" (1992) Aus.L.J. 67, reviews the standing of the *Bolam* principle in Australia, and criticises *Rogers* as introducing an anomalous test for breach of a professional duty of care.

Side effects of drugs

6–117   Add to NOTE 32: *Blyth* v. *Bloomsbury H.A.* is also reported at (1993) 4 Med.L.R. 151.

(vii) Mishandling of Mentally Disturbed Patients

Prevention of self-inflicted injury and suicide

6–132   Add to end of text: The reasoning of Edmund-Davies J. in *Thorne* v. *Northern Group Hospital Management Committee* was applied by the Court of Appeal in *Gauntlett* v. *Northampton Health Authority* (December 12, 1985, unreported). In that case a mental hospital patient, whilst walking unaccompanied to the washroom, set fire to her t-shirt and sustained injuries. The Court held that even if an earlier incident involving matches had been recorded, this would probably not have led to the plaintiff being accompanied by a nurse on every occasion when she went to the washroom. The plaintiff failed both on negligence and causation.

6–133   Add to end of text: The Ontario Court of Appeal adopted similar reasoning in *Larche* v. *Ontario* (1990) 75 D.L.R. (4th) 377. The plaintiff, a patient in a minimum security psychiatric hospital, climbed onto the roof of a hospital building in search of a frisbee. He fell and suffered injuries. The hospital was held not liable. The Court considered that, despite the risk, the open setting for a minimum security psychiatric hospital was justified because of the therapeutic benefit of treatment in that setting. This case is further discussed in the supplement to Chap. 2, § 2–61.

3.—DAMAGES

(i) Remoteness

(a) *Causation*

Add to end of text: The "but for" test is often determinative of **6–138** causation, but it does not invariably yield the right answer. In *Rogers* v. *Whitaker* (1992) 3 Med.L.R. 331 the New South Wales Court of Appeal suggested the hypothetical example of a patient injured by a crashing aircraft whilst undergoing an operation. If the medical practitioner had negligently advised the operation, it might be said that "but for" such negligent advice, the plaintiff would not have been injured. Moreover, the type of damage suffered (personal injury) would have been foreseeable. However, the medical practitioner should not be held liable in that situation, since his duty does not extend to protecting patients from extraneous or fortuitous accidents. This discussion was *obiter* and was not considered by the High Court (whose decision is summarised in § 6–116B, above).

Where the injury would have occurred in any event

Add to NOTE 9: See also *Marsden* v. *Bateman* (1993) 4 Med.L.R. 181 **6–139** (brain damage in infant caused not by failure to diagnose and treat hypoglycaemia but by defective development at the foetal stage); *Egedebo* v. *Windermere District Hospital* (1993) 78 B.C.L.R. (2d) 63 (paralysis already irreversible before its cause was negligently misdiagnosed and treated); *MacWilliam* v. *Jeffrey* (1993) 127 N.B.R. (2d) 113 (condition of plaintiff's mouth was unrelated to dental work performed by the defendant dentist).

Insert new paragraphs after § 6–141:

In *Lawson* v. *Laferriere* (1991) 78 D.L.R. (4th) 609 the Supreme Court **6–141A** of Canada reviewed this issue both in the context of civil law and common law. In March 1971 the patient consulted the defendant, a cancer specialist, about a lump in her right breast. The defendant performed a biopsy, which revealed that the patient had cancer of the breast. The defendant negligently failed to inform the patient of her condition or to follow it up. In 1975 the patient's condition deteriorated and the doctors treating her confirmed the original diagnosis of cancer. The patient died in January 1978. The medical evidence indicated that, whatever treatment the patient had received since 1971, she would probably have died of cancer. The trial judge dismissed a claim by the patient's executor because causation was not established. The Quebec Court of Appeal, by a 2:1 majority, awarded the executor $50,000 for loss of the chance of a cure.

6–141B   The Supreme Court of Canada, by a majority of 6:1, allowed the defendant's appeal in part. The Court held that the patient's executor was not entitled to damages for loss of the chance of a cure; but she was entitled to damages for the distress and diminished quality of life which the patient suffered, as a result of the four-year delay in telling her of the diagnosis. Such damages were assessed at $17,500. The majority of the Court concurred with the judgment of Gonthier J. This judgment reviewed at length the civil law on damages for loss of a chance, surveying the judicial decisions and academic writings on the topic of France, Belgium and Quebec.

6–141C   Gonthier J. also reviewed more briefly the common law on this topic and noted the House of Lords' decision in *Hotson*. He concluded that the "lost chance" approach was inappropriate in all but the exceptional classical cases, such as loss of a lottery ticket. He considered that such artificial analysis should not be extended to the medical context. Instead the courts should concentrate on what injury had been caused to the individual plaintiff, such as shorter life or greater pain. Although *Lawson* is a civil law decision, it is submitted that such a well researched and reasoned decision of the Canadian Supreme Court deserves careful consideration when the issues left over by *Hotson* arise for decision in this country.

6–141D   A somewhat different view of this topic is expressed by Dr. W. Scott in "Causation in Medico-Legal Practice: A Doctor's Approach to the 'Lost Opportunity' Cases" (1992) 55 M.L.R. 521. Scott argues that the "all or none" approach is unsatisfactory because of the practical difficulty in many borderline cases of saying on which side of the 50 per cent. line the likelihoods fall. A proportionate approach would be workable. In view of the impossibility of precision, he suggests that the courts should deal in fixed bands: 10 per cent. chance, 25 per cent. chance, 33 per cent. chance and so forth. In cases which fall near the 50 per cent. borderline, justice to the parties would be much better served by adopting a proportionate approach. From a pragmatic viewpoint, this argument has considerable force. It merits serious consideration in any statutory scheme for compensation for medical accidents. But it is not accepted that this approach is open to the courts, as the common law now stands.

6–141E   In *Bolitho* v. *City and Hackney Health Authority* (unreported, December 15, 1992) Farquharson and Dillon L.JJ. applied the *Bolam* test to the issue of factual causation. A two-year-old child, hospitalised for breathing difficulties, suffered a cardiac arrest. He was revived but had suffered severe brain damage during the arrest. His parents argued that his condition was caused by negligence on the part of the defendant's

[90]

paediatric registrar in failing to attend and intubate him. Negligence on the part of the doctor in failing to attend was conceded, but it was denied that such failure had caused the child's injuries because had the registrar attended, she would not have intubated him. The majority in the Court of Appeal held that there was a responsible body of medical opinion in support of the doctor's assertion that, had she attended, she would not have intubated; that it was not the case, therefore, that no doctor of ordinary skill would have omitted to intubate the plaintiff, and accordingly, the plaintiff failed on causation. Simon Brown L.J. dissenting, considered that the ordinary tests of causation were adequate to deal with the issue. The question was not whether it would have been unreasonable for an attending doctor to intubate the plaintiff, but whether on the balance of probabilities such doctor would have intubated. The self-serving evidence of a doctor whose conduct in a hypothetical situation is in issue should be treated with caution, and an attending doctor probably would have done what she should have done. The existence of a responsible body of medical opinion against intubation in these circumstances did not prevent the court finding that, in all the circumstances, the particular plaintiff probably would have been intubated by an attending doctor.

Inadequate warning re proposed treatment

Add: Hart and Honoré discuss the merits of the two tests in *Causation* **6–144** *in the Law*, at p. 417. They come down slightly in favour of the objective test.

Add to NOTE 46: See also *Layton* v. *Westcott* (1993) 6 Alta.L.R. 91 **6–145** (Alberta Court of Queen's Bench) (reasonable plaintiff would have agreed to hysterectomy even had she been properly warned of the particular risk in her case); *Hollis* v. *Birch* (1993) 81 B.C.L.R. (2d) 1 (B.C.C.A.) (surgeon negligent in failing to warn of risk of rupture of proposed breast implantation, case remitted for further evidence of what other women did when so warned, in order to determine what a reasonable woman would have done).

(ii) Measure of Damages

Unwanted healthy child

Add to end of text: *Allen* v. *Bloomsbury Health Authority* [1993] 1 All **6–158** E.R. 651 gives helpful guidance on the quantification of damages in such cases. In this case Brooke J. awarded the costs of upbringing, which were calculated in some detail and included a sum for the mother's loss of earnings. A claim for the costs of the child's future wedding was rejected, because it was too speculative.

Unwanted handicapped child

6-159 Add to NOTE 1: The reasoning in *Salih* v. *Enfield H.A.* is strongly criticised by P. R. Glazebrook in "Unseemliness Compounded by Injustice" (1992) 51 C.L.J. 226. It is argued that such litigation is morally unacceptable. It is also argued that such an action for financial loss is not maintainable in principle, following the House of Lords' decisions in *Governors of the Peabody Donation Fund* v. *Sir Lindsay Parkinson* [1985] A.C. 210, *Caparo Industries* v. *Dickman* [1990] 2 A.C. 605 and *Murphy* v. *Brentwood D.C.* [1991] 1 A.C. 398.

Add to end of text: Different considerations arise where the plaintiff did not want a child at all and, because of the defendant's negligence, has a handicapped child. In those circumstances she should recover the normal costs of upbringing, increased because of the handicap: see *Robinson* v. *Salford Health Authority* (1992) 3 Med.L.R. 270.

INSURANCE BROKERS

1.—GENERAL

Add to NOTE 5: In *Harvest Trucking Co. Ltd.* v. *Davis* [1991] 2 Lloyd's **7–02** Rep. 638 the defendant was not registered as an insurance broker and described himself as an "insurance intermediary." Judge Diamond Q.C., sitting in the High Court, stated that although Mr. Davis' business was indistinguishable from that of a small insurance broker, "no possible criticism can be made of the fact that Mr. Davis carried on business in the way he did."

Financial Services Act 1986
Add to NOTE 12: In relation to persons authorised by the Insurance **7–04** Brokers Registration Council under Chapter 5 of the Insurance Brokers Registration Council (Conduct of Business) Rules Approval Order 1988.

(i) Duties to Client

(a) *Contractual duties*
Add to end of text: In practice, therefore, if there is an issue as to **7–07** whether the broker has obtained insurance which meets his client's instructions or requirements, the issue is not so much whether the broker was negligent as whether the insurers are liable on the policy: if they are

not, the broker will have been negligent (see, for example, *Seavision Investment S.A.* v. *Evennett, The Tiburon* [1990] 2 Lloyd's Rep. 418, discussed at § 7–27A below and *Flying Colours Film Co. Ltd.* v. *Assicurazioni Generali S.p.A.* [1993] 2 Lloyd's Rep. 184 where the argument was solely between the insurers and the brokers, the client standing on the touchline).

(b) *Duties independent of contract*

7–09 NOTE 26. *Punjab National Bank* v. *de Boinville* is now reported at [1992] 1 W.L.R. 1138.

(ii) Duties to Third Parties

(a) *Duties to insurers*

7–13 Add to NOTE 33: See also *Bos* v. *Brauer* (1992) 3 Alta.L.R. (3d) 318, where a broker coverholder was found to be in breach of duty in failing to provide accurate information to insurers. However, since there was no evidence that insurers would have acted differently had they received accurate information, they recovered only nominal damages.

7–15 NOTE 41. The decision of the House of Lords in *Bank of Nova Scotia* v. *Hellenic Mutual War Risks Association (Bermuda) Ltd., The Good Luck* is now reported at [1992] 1 A.C. 233.

(b) *Duties to other third parties*

7–19 NOTE 46. *Punjab National Bank* v. *de Boinville* is now reported at [1992] 1 W.L.R. 1138.

7–20 NOTE 48. *Punjab National Bank* v. *de Boinville* is now reported at [1992] 1 W.L.R. 1138.

Add to end of text: In *Verderame* v. *Commercial Union Assurance Co. plc* [1992] BCLC 793 the sole directors and shareholders of a limited company who were in effect carrying on business through the medium of the company in quasi partnership brought a claim in tort against the company's insurance brokers claiming, *inter alia*, damages for losses allegedly suffered by them personally. Their case was that their company had been unable to continue trading when it did not receive an indemnity from insurers after suffering a loss and that they had thereby personally suffered a loss of income. The Court of Appeal adopted the incremental approach advocated by Brennan J. in *Sutherland Shire Council* v. *Heyman* (1985) 60 A.L.R. 1, 43–44 and approved by the House of Lords in *Caparo Industries plc* v. *Dickman* [1990] 2 A.C. 605 and struck out this claim as disclosing no reasonable cause of action. Apart from the fact that such a duty would be contrary to the basic principles of company law set out in the leading case of *Salomon* v. *Salomon Ltd.* [1897] A.C. 22 and that it would allow directors to circumvent the rules governing the winding up of companies, there was no recognised category where such a duty had been held to exist and the Court of Appeal held that it would not be a justifiable increment to any existing category to accept the existence of such a duty.

(iii) The Standard of Skill and Care

Add to end of text: In *Sharp and Roarer Investments Ltd.* v. *Sphere* **7–21** *Drake Insurance plc, The Moonacre* [1992] 2 Lloyd's Rep. 501 (for the facts see § 7–35, below) A.D. Colman Q.C., sitting as a deputy judge of the High Court, had to consider the standard of skill required of an insurance broker who undertook to obtain insurance for a yacht when considering whether a broker had been negligent in relation to a particular clause of a marine insurance policy. He referred to *Duchess of Argyll* v. *Beuselinck* [1972] 2 Lloyd's Rep. 172 (see Chap. 1, § 1–70 and Chap. 4, § 4–52) and said at p. 523, column 2:

"In deciding whether their standard of skill was sufficiently high, it is appropriate . . . to require that a non-specialist marine broker should bear no greater skill than that which would be expected from a reasonably skilled non-specialist broker. This is not the same thing as saying that the standard is that of a marine broker substantially inexperienced in the insurance of large yachts. It is rather the standard of a broker who has such general knowledge of the yacht insurance market and the cover available in it as to be able to advise his client on all matters on which a lay client would in the ordinary course of events predictably need advice, in particular in the course of the selection of cover and the completion of the proposal."

In other words, where a broker undertakes work in a specialist market, he will be required to exercise reasonable skill and care in the context of that market.

2.—LIABILITY FOR BREACH OF DUTY

(i) Failing to Effect Insurance

NOTE 72: *Cosyns* v. *Smith* is also reported at 146 D.L.R. (3d) 622.   **7–26**

Insert new paragraph after § 7–27:

In *Seavision Investment S.A.* v. *Evennett, The Tiburon* [1990] 2 Lloyd's **7–27A** Rep. 418, brokers had purported to place war risks cover for a ship owned by a Panamanian company under an open cover for ships in German ownership. A loss was suffered and one underwriter denied liability on the basis that the owner was not German so that the risk did not fall within the terms of the open cover. The owner brought proceedings against both the underwriter and the brokers. The brokers conceded at trial that if the underwriter was not liable, they were, a concession which Steyn J. said "anticipated what would have been an inevitable conclusion." He went on to find that the underwriter was not liable and gave judgment against the brokers.

(ii) Effecting Insurance, But Not on the Terms Specified by the Client

7–29   Add to end of text: A broker who is instructed by various companies in the same group to arrange insurance for their respective properties will be in breach of duty to the company which owns a particular property if, despite being informed that that company owns the property, he obtains insurance for that property in the name of a different company: *Austcan Investments Pty. Ltd.* v. *Sun Alliance Insurance Ltd.* (1992) 57 S.A.S.R. 343 at first instance (on appeal, *ibid.*, it was held that the correct company had been insured, but that the broker had been negligent in another respect: see § 7–47, below).

Add to NOTE 85: See also *McNicol* v. *Insurance Unlimited (Calgary) Ltd.* (1992) 5 Alta.L.R. (3d) 158: a broker instructed to obtain insurance against ice hazards negligently obtained a policy which excluded cover for damage caused by floods.

(iii) Effecting Insurance which does not Meet the Client's Requirements

7–32   Add to NOTE 96: See also *Mitzner* v. *Miller & Beazley Ltd.* (1993) 11 Alta.L.R. (3d) 108: broker held liable for not properly investigating his client's requirements so that the policy procured did not cover loss and damage to tools.

Add NOTE 99a at end of paragraph: In *Dallinga* v. *Sun Alliance Insurance Co.* (1993) 10 Alta.L.R. (3d) 59 the owner of goods stored at his son's property arranged contents cover for his son through the defendant broker. He did not tell the broker that the goods were his. They were stolen. The son had no insurable interest and the father was not named on the policy, so neither could claim for the loss. The broker had no reason to believe that the goods were the father's property and the claim against him was dismissed.

7–33   Add to end of text: A client who is informed of possible coverage but decides not to obtain it cannot complain if he then suffers a loss which would have been covered: *Davca Building Supplies Ltd.* v. *Wedgewood*

Insurance Ltd. and Clarke (1992) 99 Nfld. & P.E.I.R. 203. (The client was informed of possible cover in respect of liability for damage to trailers towed by his truck but chose not to obtain it. His action against the broker failed.)

Add to end of text: The facts of *Strong & Pearl* v. *S. Allison & Co.* **7–35** *Ltd.* (1926) 25 Ll.L.Rep. 504 bear a resemblance to those in the more recent decision of A.D. Colman Q.C., sitting as a Deputy Judge of the High Court in *Sharp and Roarer Investments Ltd.* v. *Sphere Drake Insurance plc, The Moonacre* [1992] 2 Lloyd's Rep. 501. In the latter case brokers were held to have been negligent in arranging insurance for a yacht on terms which included an exclusion of cover for any period when the yacht was used as a houseboat. The insured's crew lived on his yacht when it was laid up over winter and this allowed insurers to rely upon the exclusion when a loss occurred. When preparing the proposal form the broker had asked whether the insured or his family would live on the yacht over winter, but failed to ask whether anyone else would. He was therefore held to have been negligent.

(v) Failing to Act with Reasonable Speed

Add to NOTE 17: In *Icarom plc (formerly Insurance Corporation of* **7–39** *Ireland plc)* v. *Peek Puckle (International) Ltd.* [1992] 2 Lloyd's Rep. 600 the plaintiff alleged that the defendant broker, having been instructed on January 19, had been negligent in failing to obtain facultative reinsurance cover until January 22, by when a total loss had occurred on the underlying policy. Webster J. held that the brokers had only been instructed on the 22nd, so that the claim failed on its facts. It appears to have been considered to be at least arguable that the brokers would have been negligent had they taken four days to obtain reinsurance cover.

Add to end of text: In *Labreche Estate* v. *Harasymiw* (1992) 89 D.L.R. (4th) 95 an employee of a credit union who assisted a mortgagor in applying for life insurance was held to be in breach of a tortious duty of care in taking three months to cmplete an application form and generally failing to progress the application.

(vi) Failing to Disclose Material Facts to the Insurers

Add to end of text: In *Pan Atlantic Insurance Co. Ltd.* v. *Pine Top* **7–40** *Insurance Co. Ltd.* [1993] 1 Lloyd's Rep. 496 the Court of Appeal explained that the test is whether a prudent insurer would view the undisclosed material as probably tending to increase the risk.

Add to end of text: The fact that the broker has forged his client's **7–41** signature on the proposal form is a material fact even if the client would have readily signed the form as completed himself. In *Sharp and Roarer Investments Ltd.* v. *Sphere Drake Insurance plc, The Moonacre* [1992] 2 Lloyd's Rep. 501 a broker who did so without authority was held liable when insurers avoided cover for non-disclosure.

(vii) Making a Misrepresentation to the Insurers

7–43   Add NOTE 36a at end of paragraph: In *Rivard* v. *Mutual Life Insurance Co. of Canada* (1992) 9 O.R. (3d) 545 (Ontario Court (General Division)) an insurance agent was held to have been in breach of duty to an intended beneficiary of a policy of life insurance for allowing the person whose life was to be insured to represent falsely that he had never smoked. The misrepresentation was unequivocal and the basis upon which the agent (who had some reason to question what was said) was held negligent is not clear. Yates J. appears to have applied a particularly rigorous standard of care.

7–44   Add to end of text: A broker who forges his client's signature on the proposal form without his client's authority will thereby make a misrepresentation to insurers and be in breach of duty to his client: *Sharp and Roarer Investments Ltd.* v. *Sphere Drake Insurance plc, The Moonacre* [1992] 2 Lloyd's Rep. 501.

(viii) Failing to Keep the Client Properly Informed

7–47   Add to end of text: If a broker fails to send a copy of the policy to his client, he may fall under a duty to advise the client of any important policy conditions. Thus in *Austcan Investments Pty. Ltd.* v. *Sun Alliance Insurance Ltd.* (1992) 57 S.A.S.R. 343 brokers were held to have assumed a duty to advise their client of a clause whereby the policy was avoided if there was a change of use of the insured premises during the policy period unless agreed by insurers.

Renewal
7–48   NOTE 56. *Harvest Trucking Co. Ltd.* v. *Davis* is now reported at [1991] 2 Lloyd's Rep. 638.

(ix) Failing to Give Proper Advice

7–51   Add to NOTE 63: *Random Ford Mercury Sales Ltd.* v. *Noseworthy* (1992) 95 D.L.R. (4th) 168: agent negligently advising unpaid vendor of boat that his interest was covered under insurance arranged for the purchaser. Seller allowed purchaser to take boat which was lost. Broker liable.

Add to NOTE 71: In *Sharp and Roarer Investments Ltd.* v. *Sphere Drake Insurance plc, The Moonacre* [1992] 2 Lloyd's Rep. 501 (for the facts see § 7–35, above) another basis of the broker's liability was failure to give accurate advice as to the true meaning of the particular exclusion clause.

Add NOTE 72a at end of the paragraph: See also *Fletcher* v. *Manitoba Public Insurance Co.* (1990) 74 D.L.R. (4th) 636: public insurance corporation held to be in breach of tortious duty of care in failing to advise insured of availability and importance of underinsured motorist coverage.

NOTE 78: See also *Sharp and Roarer Investments Ltd.* v. *Sphere Drake*   7–54
Insurance plc, The Moonacre [1992] 2 Lloyd's Rep. 501 (for the relevant facts see § 7–35, above). In finding the broker negligent in relation to the houseboat exclusion clause A. D. Colman Q.C. said at p. 525, column 2: "If there was any doubt in [the broker's] mind as to the matter it was the duty of the broker to ask the insurers . . . what meaning they attached to the question and the houseboat exclusion."

3.—DAMAGES

(ii) Measure of Damages

Add to end of text: Where insurers make an *ex gratia* payment, credit   7–75
should be given for it: *Harvest Trucking Co. Ltd.* v. *Davis* [1991] 2 Lloyd's Rep. 638.

Add to end of text: In *Verderame* v. *Commercial Union Assurance Co.*   7–76
plc [1992] BCLC 793 (for the facts see § 7–20, above), the Court of Appeal followed *Ramwade Ltd.* v. *W. J. Emson & Co. Ltd.* [1987] R.T.R. 72 and held that losses alleged to have been caused by failure to receive promptly monies under an insurance policy were irrecoverable in tort. This paragraph should be read with Chapter 3, § 3–156.

Add to NOTE 36: In *Sharp and Roarer Investments Ltd.* v. *Sphere*   7–77
Drake Insurance plc, The Moonacre [1992] 2 Lloyd's Rep. 501 A.D. Colman Q.C., sitting as a deputy judge of the High Court, appeared to consider it appropriate to give credit for returned premium, although he left the point open for further argument.

Add to NOTE 40: In *Seavision Investment S.A.* v. *Evennett, The*   7–78
Tiburon (for the facts of the underlying trial see § 7–27A, above) Steyn J., when considering the basis upon which the brokers should pay the plaintiff's costs of suing the underwriter, said that he derived little

assistance from the older cases and awarded costs taxed on the standard basis, rather than on a solicitor and own client or indemnity basis. His judgment on this point is not reported at first instance, but the plaintiff sought to appeal and the relevant part is set out in the judgments of the Court of Appeal: *Seavision Investment S.A.* v. *Evennett, The Tiburon* [1992] 2 Lloyd's Rep. 26. The Court of Appeal held that pursuant to section 18(1)(*f*) of the Supreme Court Act 1981, it had no jurisdiction to entertain an appeal on the question of costs alone because Steyn J. had refused leave to appeal. However, Parker L.J. expressed "considerable doubt" as to Steyn J.'s decision.

7–80 Add to end of text: In *Verderame* v. *Commercial Union Assurance Co. plc* [1992] BCLC 793 (for the facts see § 7–20, above) the directors claimed damages for anxiety, depression and inconvenience. The Court of Appeal held that such damages would not be recoverable against a broker in contract and therefore should not be recoverable in tort.

(iii) Contributory Negligence

7–81 NOTE 45. *Cosyns* v. *Smith* is also reported at 146 D.L.R. (3d) 622.

7–82 Add to NOTE 52: His decision was upheld by the Court of Appeal: [1992] 2 Lloyd's Rep. 127.

7–84 Add to NOTE 60: And in *Labreche Estate* v. *Harasymiw* (1992) 89 D.L.R. (4th) 95 (for the facts see § 7–39, above) the mortgagor was held to have been 50 per cent. negligent for failing to respond in a timely manner to requests from the potential insurers for further information which he should have known they would require before granting cover.

Insert new paragraph after § 7–84:

7–84A The position is different where the alleged contributory negligence is failure by a client without any expertise to realise that the broker had failed to appreciate the purpose and effect of a particular clause of the policy. Thus in *Sharp and Roarer Investments Ltd.* v. *Sphere Drake Insurance plc, The Moonacre* [1992] 2 Lloyd's Rep. 501 (for the relevant facts see § 7–35, above) the argument that the client should have appreciated the effect of the houseboat exclusion clause was rejected as "entirely misconceived."

ACCOUNTANTS

1.—GENERAL

(ii) Duties to Client

(a) *Contractual duties*

Add to NOTE 68: Note *Roman Corporation Ltd.* v. *Peat Marwick* **8–15** *Thorne* (1922) 8 B.L.R. 43 (Ontario Court of Justice, Farley J.): although shareholders are entitled by resolution to appoint and remove auditors, that does not give rise to a contract between them (as distinct from the company) and the auditors.

(a) *Fiduciary duties*

Add to end of paragraph: In *Hodgkinson* v. *Simms*[29a] the British **8–23** Columbia Court of Appeal reversed the trial judge's finding that the defendant accountant owed a fiduciary duty to the plaintiff on the basis that such a duty must arise out of the relationship of the parties prior to the breach and not out of the conduct of the fiduciary in the breach.[29b]

NOTE 29a. (1992) 65 B.C.L.R. (2d) 264.

NOTE 29b. The defendant was held to have been under a contractual duty to disclose material information and to have been in breach by failing to disclose a relationship with the developers of the housing investment in which the plaintiff had invested, whereby the accountant derived fees and other payments for services rendered.

(iii) Duties to Third Parties

(a) *Pre-Caparo case law*

8–39 Add to NOTE 78: The reasonable foresight test was also applied in the Irish case of *Kelly* v. *Boland* [1989] I.R.L.M. 373. although the claim failed on other grounds.

(b) *Caparo Industries plc* v. *Dickman*

Insert new paragraph after § 8–49:

8–49A Claims by equity investors have been considered in various overseas jurisdiction since *Caparo*. In a Canadian case, *Roman Corporation Ltd.* v. *Peat Marwick Thorne,* [94a] the judge held that the defendant auditors owed no duty of care to plaintiffs as sharcholders even though they may have been controlling shareholders. *Caparo* has also been followed in Singapore.[94b] In an Australian case, *Columbia Coffee & Tea Pty Ltd.* v. *Churchill,* [94c] Rolfe J. considered that there was an assumption of responsibility on the part of the defendant auditors such as to bring the plaintiff purchaser of shares within the class of persons whom a duty of care was owed. This conclusion was based primarily on a statement in the auditors' audit manual expressly "acknowledg[ing] that there will be interested parties who read and rely upon our reports, and this extends beyond the persons who employ us in the first instance or those to whom the report is addressed initially." The plaintiff was unable, however, to demonstrate reliance on the relevant audited accounts and the claim failed.

NOTE 94A. (1992) 8 B.L.R. 43. (Ontario Court of Justice). The judge (at p. 56) referred to previous decisions (*Queen* v. *Cognos Inc.* (1990) 74 O.R. (2d) 176 and *Roncato* v. *Caverly* (1991) 84 D.L.R. 303) in which the Ontario Court of Appeal "have applied the *Caparo* decision indicating that recovery in cases of negligent misrepresentation is limited to situations where economic loss resulted from *detrimental* reliance upon negligent missstatements to a *known* recipient (either as an individual or a member of an identifiable class) for a *specific* purpose. See *Cognos* at p. 182 and *Roncato* at p. 721."

NOTE 94b. *Ikumene Singapore Pte Ltd.* v. *Leong Chee Leng* [1992] 2 S.L.R. 891 (Goh Joon Seng J. at first instance); [1993] 3 S.L.R. 24 (Court of Appeal). Claims by a shareholder and guarantor were dismissed.

NOTE 94c. (1992) 29 N.S.W.L.R. 141.

(c) *Third party claimants other than equity investors*

8–50 In *Huxford* v. *Stoy Hayward*, the judge was Popplewell J. not Otton J.

Add to NOTE 2: Note *Al Saudi* has been followed in rejecting an **8–51**
alleged duty of care in Australia, see *R. Lowe Lippman Figdor & Franck*
v. *A.G.C. (Advances) Ltd.* [1992] 2 V.R. 661 (Supreme Court of
Victoria, Appeal Division); in Canada, see *Rangen Inc.* v. *Deloitte &
Touche* (1993) 79 B.C.L.R. 31 and *Canadian Commercial Bank* v.
Crawford Smith & Swallow (1993) 9 B.L.R. 311; and in Singapore, see
Ikumene Singapore Pte Ltd. v. *Leong Chee Leng* [1993] 3 S.L.R. 24,
C.A. *Cf. Salberg* v. *Touche, Ross & Co.* (1993) 81 B.C.L.R. 365
(B.C.C.A.) in which a guarantor's claim succeeded.

Insert new paragraphs after § 8–52:

In *Berg Sons & Co. Ltd.* v. *Mervyn Hampton Adams*[13a] the scope of an **8–52A**
auditor's duty of care was explored in the context of claims arising from
the collapse of a fraudulent "one man" company. G controlled the
company as effectively the sole shareholder and director. His was "the
directing mind and will of the company" and "his knowledge was the
company's knowledge." Assisted by certain banks, the company engaged
in bill discounting activities with the underlying purpose of the provision
of credit. Following the company's collapse in 1985 with a deficiency of
£15.5m, its auditors were sued in contract by the company and in tort by
certain banks arising from the auditors' statutory audit and report upon
the company's 1982 accounts some two years previously. It was not
alleged that any director or shareholder was misled by, or relied on,
anything said or done by the auditors or that G was not fully aware of all
relevant facts and considerations. Hobhouse J. dismissed the claims. As
to the company's claim, although the auditors were in breach of contract
in not qualifying their report for uncertainty in respect of the
recoverability of certain bills of exchange, no loss was caused thereby. As
to the banks' claim, the judge proceeded from an analysis of *Caparo* to
reject the duty of care asserted by them. He did so notwithstanding a
letter written by the auditors to G indicating actual foresight of reliance
on the audited accounts by the company's banks and the auditors' view
that any such bank suffering loss on the company's insolvency would have
a claim against them. The purpose of a statutory audit[13b] was:

> " . . . to provide a mechanism to enable those having a proprietary
> interest in the company or being concerned with its management
> or control to have access to accurate financial information about
> the company. Provided that those persons have that informa-
> tion, the statutory purpose is exhausted. What those persons do with
> the information is a matter for them and falls outside the scope of the
> statutory purpose. In the present case the [company] based [its] case
> not upon any lack of information on the part of [G] but rather upon

the opportunity that the possession of the auditor's certificate is said to have given for the company to continue to carry on business and to borrow money from third parties. Such matters do not fall within the scope of the duty of the statutory auditor."[13c]

NOTE 13a. (1992) 8 P.N. 167.
NOTE 13b. *I.e.* under the Companies Acts.
NOTE 13c. (1992) 8 P.N. 167, 178.

8–52B   New Zealand courts both at first instance and on appeal in *Fletcher* v. *National Mutual Life Nominees Ltd.*,[13d] held that the relationship between auditors and a third party trustee was sufficiently proximate as to support a duty of care. However, on further appeal to the Privy Council *sub nom.* *Deloitte Haskins & Sells* v. *National Mutual Life Nominees Ltd.*,[13e] the auditors succeeded in reversing this finding. The Privy Council concluded that the statutory context negated a duty of the scope contended for by the trustee.

NOTE 13d. [1990] 3 N.Z.L.R. 641 (first instance); 1991 N.Z.B.L.C. 102, 259, C.A.
NOTE 13e. [1993] 2 All E.R. 1015.

8–52C   The facts were that a company which operated as a wholesale money market dealer, obtained deposits from the public by a prospectus issue. An independent trustee was appointed for the protection of the unsecured depositors. Under the trust deed, the company was restricted from entering transactions with any associated company and agreed not to permit its liabilities to exceed certain limits. It also agreed to provide regular reports to the trustee together with a separate report from its auditors stating that they had received the directors' report and had no reason to believe that the statements in the report were not correct. The company and the trustee were parties to the trust deed, but the auditors were not.

8–52D   Under section 50(2) of the New Zealand Securities Act 1978 an auditor was required to provide a report to the company and a copy to the trustee or "statutory supervisor," "[w]henever, in the performance of his duties as an auditor, the auditor of an issuer of debt securities . . . offered to the public becomes aware of any matter that in his opinion is relevant to the exercise or performance of the powers or duties of the trustee or statutory supervisor of the securities." The company developed liquidity problems arising from a series of unsecured loans between it and other companies within the same group. Eventually, concern as to the collectability of certain loans prompted the auditors to issue a section 50(2) report to the company and the trustee. Shortly afterwards the company went into liquidation and was unable to meet its liabilities to unsecured depositors. A representative claim by an unsecured depositor against the trustee was settled. The trustee then sought recovery from the directors and auditors on the basis of alleged duties of care owed to the trustee.

Henry J. at first instance held both the auditors and directors were **8–52E** liable. In relation to the auditors he attached particular importance to the investor protection aim of the Act and held that the auditors were in breach of a duty of care owed to the trustees in not forming an opinion at an earlier stage on matters bearing on the probable insolvency of the company. His decision was upheld by the New Zealand Court of Appeal.

The Privy Council reasoned that such a common law duty could not be **8–52F** justified when such a duty could not be supported as a matter of statutory intention. The statutory duty to report only arose after the auditor became aware of what was a relevant matter "in his opinion," a term suggesting the application of a subjective test. Contrasting the relevant section with the New Zealand equivalent to section 237(1) of the English Companies Act 1985,[13f] Lord Jauncey continued:

> "Under the latter section a positive duty is imposed on auditors to make a report in which they express an opinion, from which it follows that a failure to form an opinion could constitute a breach of a common law duty owed to the members. However, under the former section the only positive duty on an auditor is to send timeously a report after he has become aware of a particular matter and has formed an opinion that it is relevant to the exercise of the powers or duties of a trustee. The duty to report is accordingly contingent and the only omission by the auditor which can at common law give rise to a breach of duty is failure to exercise reasonable care in the preparation of such report when the circumstances requiring its making have arisen."[13g]

The Privy Council also held that the trustee had failed to discharge the burden upon it of establishing that any breach of duty by the auditors had caused it loss. The evidence suggested that even if they had reported earlier the trustee would have had to suspend the operations of the company, leading to a run on the company by depositors and liability on the part of the trustee to the same extent as that actually incurred by it following the auditors' actual later report.

NOTE 13f. See § 8–08, above.

NOTE 13g. [1993] 2 All E.R. 1015 at p. 1023.

(d) *Liabilities arising from reports listing particulars and company prospectuses*

Insert new paragraph after § 8–53:

8-53A   The above analysis is borne out by the Canadian case of *Kripps* v. *Touche Ross & Co.*[17a] which contains a refreshingly succinct analysis of possible bases for a duty of care and of the circumstances in which an accountant may incur liability in tort to investors arising from opinions expressed in an offer document. Some 560 holders of debentures in a failed mortgage company sought to recover their losses from a firm of accountants. They maintained that the debentures would not have been offered to the public if the accountants had not been negligent in respect of audit reports which they had consented to be included in the required prospectuses. The accountants applied to strike out the claim. In support of the contention that the accountants owed them a duty of care, the plaintiffs alleged that they actually relied on the financial statements or, alternatively, that they were entitled to a legal presumption of reliance based on a U.S. doctrine known as "Reliance on the Integrity of the Market" or a variation on that doctrine contemplating reliance on the regulatory system. The effect of these doctrines was described by the court as to "obviate the need for proof of reliance on a particular defendant in stock market cases so long as it can be said that securities of the sort in question would not get onto the market without scrutiny, and that the security in question would not have passed scrutiny had the defendant acted carefully."[17b] The British Columbia Court of Appeal, upholding the judge at the first instance, rejected such doctrines and struck out allegations based on deemed reliance, but refused to strike out allegations based on actual reliance.[17c]

NOTE 17a. (1992) 69 B.C.L.R. (2d) 62.

NOTE 17b. *Ibid.* at p. 85.

NOTE 17c. The investors' claims against the Superintendent of Brokers, the relevant regulator under the British Columbian Securities Act 1979, were also struck out.

(iv) The Standard of Skill and Care

(a) *The standard of reasonableness*

8-60   Add to NOTE 52: But note *AWA Ltd.* v. *Daniels t/a Deloitte Haskins & Sells* (1992) 7 A.C.S.R. 759. The judge upheld the plaintiff's contention that it was the auditors duty timeously to report on deficiencies in internal control to senior management and, if they failed to act, to the board of directors. The auditors were in breach of duty in failing to do so sufficiently promptly.

8-61   Add to NOTE 60: See also now *AWA Ltd.* v. *Daniels t/a Deloitte Haskins & Sells* (1992) 7 A.C.S.R. 759. Specialist experience may be required of an auditor: see the same case at p. 775, "If ever there was ample reason for calling in [an auditor specialising in foreign exchange transactions] this was it."

(c) *General practice and knowledge as evidence of the standard*

Add after second sentence: Reflecting similar statements in other **8-63** professional negligence cases, the Alberta Court of Appeal in dismissing a claim against accountants in *Sceptre Resources Ltd.* v. *Deloitte Haskins & Sells*,[80a] proceeded from the premises that:

> "The law allows differing opinions among accountants as it does within the medical and legal professions. Acting in concert with an opinion or practice held by a significant fraction of the profession, is almost always a defence to a suit for malpractice . . . The only exception arises where the practice of the profession is totally unreasonable."[80b]

NOTE 80a. (1991) 83 Alta L.R. (2d) 157: claim for alleged misclassification of future equipment rentals in performing a certification function in relation to a corporate reorganisation. The accountants' treatment of the rentals did not contravene "any established monolithic professional view or custom and may even have represented the better view."

NOTE 80b. *Ibid.* at pp. 165–166.

Add to end of text: The full texts of all U.K. auditing standards and **8-64** guidelines and of U.K. accounting standards and of relevant exposure drafts are published annually by the Institute of Chartered Accountants. For those extant at April 1993, see *Auditing and Reporting 1993/94* and *Accounting Standards 1993/94* respectively. Latest texts are published in *Accountancy,* a monthly publication.

(v) Relief from Liability

Add at end of paragraph: However, a different view was taken by **8-67** Rogers C.J. in a more recent New South Wales case, *AWA Ltd.* v. *Daniels t/a Deloitte Haskins & Sells.*[11a] He concluded that the relevant provision was an appropriate provision for allocation of fault. He made an alternative finding that if he were wrong in his view that the defence of contributory negligence was available to the defendant auditors "the same facts, in my view, would enliven the operation of the provisions of the section."[11b]

NOTE 11a. (1992) 7 A.C.S.R. 759.

NOTE 11b. *Ibid.* at p. 856.

2.—LIABILITY FOR BREACH OF DUTY

(ii) Inadequate Ascertainment of Enterprise's Accounting System and Improper Reliance on Internal Controls

Add to NOTE 37: See also the extensive discussion of internal control in **8-76** *AWA Ltd.* v. *Daniels t/a Deloitte Haskins & Sells* (1992) 7 A.C.S.R. 759

especially at pp. 796–802 and at pp. 834–835. The judge upheld the plaintiff's contention that it was the auditors' duty timeously to report in deficiencies in internal control to senior management and, if they failed to act, to the board of directors. The auditors were in breach of duty in failing to do so sufficiently promptly.

(iii) Failing to Obtain Relevant and Reliable Audit Evidence

Unauthorised transactions

8–89   Add before first sentence: Insofar as there is any doubt in the mind of an auditor as to the scope of the authority of a member of staff, including as to whether there was any limitation on it, he should make the necessary inquiries.[95a]

NOTE 95a: See *AWA Ltd.* v. *Daniels t/a Deloitte Haskins & Sells* (1992) 7 A.C.S.R. 759 at p. 787.

(vi) Inaccurate Advice

8–99   Add at the very end of the paragraph NOTE 40a: In the Canadian case of *Roncato* v. *Caverly* (1991) 84 D.L.R. 303, the defendant accountant in recommending a book-keeper to the plaintiff company, negligently misrepresented her qualifications. The book-keeper proved dishonest. However, the Ontario Court of Appeal held that the plaintiff had failed to establish that the negligence was the cause of the claimed loss.

3.—DAMAGES

(i) Remoteness

(a) *Causation*

8–102   Add to NOTE 51: Failure to establish causation has been fatal to claims in several recent overseas claims: in Australia, see *Columbia Coffee & Tea Pty Ltd.* v. *Churchill; Saunders* v. *Donyoke Pty Ltd.* (1992) 29 N.S.W.L.R. 141 (no reliance); in Canada, see *Flandro* v. *Mitha* (1992) 7 B.L.R. 280 (no reliance); arising from New Zealand *Deloitte Haskins & Sells* v. *National Mutual Life Nominees Ltd.* [1993] 2 All E.R. 1015, P.C.; in South Africa, *International Shipping Co. (Pty.) Ltd.* v. *Bentley* 1990 (1) S.A. 680.

Add at end of paragraph: In *Berg Sons & Co. Ltd.* v. *Mervyn Hampton Adams*,[56a] although the defendant auditors were held in breach of contract in relation to the plaintiff "one man" company, there were a number of insuperable obstacles to establishing causation. Fatal to the contention that the company was misled was the complete control of G:

"There was no entity which it can be said he misled or in relation to which it can be said that he was acting fraudulently in relation to the audit in October 1982. However one identifies the company, whether it is the head management, or the company in general meeting, it was not misled and no fraud was practised upon it. This is a simple and unsurprising consequence of the fact that every physical manifestation of the company Berg was [G] himself. Any company must in the last resort, if it is to allege that it was fraudulently misled, be able to point to some natural person who was not misled by the fraud. That the Plaintiffs cannot do."[56b]

NOTE 56a. (1992) 8 P.N. 167: for facts, see § 8–52A, above.

NOTE 56b. *Ibid.* at p. 178, *per* Hobhouse J.

Contributory negligence

Insert new paragraph after § 8–104:

Extensive consideration to the defence of contributory negligence in **8–104A** the context of inadequate internal control is given by Roger C.J. in the New South Wales case of *AWA Ltd.* v. *Daniels t/a Deloitte Haskins & Sells.*[67a] Vast losses were incurred by a company as a consequence of foreign exchange hedging transactions by an employee. Severe deficiencies in the system of internal control resulted in the losses being concealed from the company's directors. The company sued its auditors alleging that its loss was caused by their negligence in respect of two audits. In particular the company contended that the auditors were negligent in failing to report the company's foreign exchange exposure and deficiencies in the accounting records and the system of internal control. The auditors denied liability, alleged contributory negligence on the part of the company and sought relief from liability under the Australian equivalent to section 727 of the Companies Act 1985. Further they made cross-claims (*i.e.* contribution claims) against the directors and banks who had advanced loans to facilitate the foreign exchange transactions. Rogers C.J. held that the auditors were negligent in the respects alleged against it, the company was contributorily negligent and its chairman and chief executive was liable on the cross-claim. The auditor's cross-claims against the non-executive directors and the banks failed. As to apportionment of liability, the judge held that the auditors had a right to elect whether to have the chairman's negligence taken into account as part of the company's contributory negligence or to claim contribution from him as a concurrent tortfeasor. The auditors elected the latter. The judge reduced the company's claim by 20 per cent. on account of contributory negligence on the part of its senior management and ordered the chairman to make a contribution to the auditors of 10 per cent. of the 80 per cent. of the loss remaining after the 20 per cent. deduction for the company's contributory negligence.

[109]

NOTE 67a. (1992) 7 A.C.S.R. 759 (interim judgment on liability); (1992) 9 A.C.S.R. 383 (judgment mainly on apportionment of liability).

8–104B   The judgment contains a detailed consideration of internal control [67b] and of the defence of contributory negligence in a company's claim against an auditor."[67c] Following a review of the organisation of large corporations, relevant case law and articles, including on imputability theory, the judge concluded that the person whose fault is to be imputed to a corporation need not be a director but may be a member of senior management. He held that there was contributory negligence on the part of the company through its senior management in several respects, including failures to employ a specialist and experienced foreign exchange managers, to establish a proper structure of internal controls, to report deficiencies in such control to the board and to supervise the employee directly responsible for the relevant hedging transactions:

> "I believe it is useful, at this point, to highlight some of the difficulties which seem to me to arise in the allocation of liability for the state of affairs I have recounted . . . Foremost among these is the failure to recognise and to admit that many companies today are too big to be supervised and administered by a board of directors except in relation to matters of high policy. The true oversight of the activities of such companies resides with the corporate bureaucracy. Senior management and, in the case of mammoth corporations, even persons lower down the corporate ladder exercise substantial control over the activities of such corporations involving important decisions and much money. It is something of an anachronism to expect non-executive directors, meeting once a month, to contribute anything much more than decisions on questions of policy and, in the case of really large corporations, only major policy. This necessarily means that, in the execution of policy, senior management is in the true sense of the word exercising the powers of decision and of management which in less complex days used to be reserved for the board of directors.[67d]

NOTE 67b. (1992) 7 A.C.S.R. 759 especially at pp. 796–802 and at pp. 834–835.

NOTE 67c. *Ibid.* at pp. 832–834 and pp. 841–854.

NOTE 67d. *Ibid.* at p. 832.

8–104C   The judge rejected a dichotomy between the board of directors and management, such as to identify only the former with the company and thus to absolve the company of contributory negligence in respect of a function of management (foreign exchange trading) and not the board.[67e] He also rejected the plaintiff's case:

". . . that, even though it would seem that senior management had permitted Koval to conduct the company's FX trading with complete lack of supervision, without regard to elemental principles of internal control, without a proper system of books and record, none of that should be taken into account in allocating fault because it was the duty of the auditors to draw to the attention of the board of directors the failure of management to maintain proper records and to implement proper principles in internal control. I cannot accept that a corporation is entitled to abdicate all responsibility for proper management of the financial aspects of its operation and then, when loss is suffered, to seek to attribute the entirety of blame to auditors."[67f]

He cited in support passages from the (then draft) report of the Committee on the Financial Aspects of Corporate Governance (the Cadbury Report) asserting the responsibility of directors to maintain a system of internal control.

NOTE 67e. (1992) 7 A.C.S.R. 759 at p. 833; also at p. 852 " . . . in the present case there is every economic reason for identifying the plaintiff corporation with the negligent acts of its senior management."

NOTE 67f. *Ibid.* at pp. 833–834.

(ii) Measure of Damages

Insert new paragraph after § 8–108:

Double recovery

In assessing damages, avoidance of double recovery may preclude a **8–108A** shareholder succeeding in a claim against an auditor of a company in circumstances where the company also sues. Recovery by the company of damages against the auditor may restore both the company and, indirectly the shareholder, to the position which each would have occupied but for the relevant breach of contract or negligence.[77a]

NOTE 77a. See the concession to this effect in the Australian case of *Columbia Coffee & Tea Pty. Ltd.* v. *Churchill; Saunders* v. *Donyoke Pty Ltd.* (1992) 29 N.S.W.L.R. 141 at pp. 157 and 173. In the event the shareholder's claim failed owing to failure to establish reliance: see § 8–49A, above.